Citizenship in Action

2

FRANK GALLIGAN
ANDY GRIFFITH
PETER NORTON
ANNE RILEY

Heinemann Educational Publishers
Halley Court, Jordan Hill, Oxford OX2 8EJ
a division of Harcourt Education Limited

Heinemann is a registered trademark of
Harcourt Education Limited

(c) Frank Galligan, Andy Griffith, Peter Norton, Anne Riley, 2003

First published 2003

07 06
10 9 8 7 6 5

British Library Cataloguing in Publication Data is available
from the British Library on request.

10 digit ISBN 0 435 808 036
13 digit ISBN 978 0 435808 03 7

Designed by Tony Richardson
Produced by Wooden Ark (Leeds)
Original illustrations (c) Harcourt Education Limited, 2002
Illustrated by Joan Corlass, Phil Burrows, Tony Richardson,
Margaret Jones, The Art Business
Printed and bound in China by Everbest
Cover photo: (Woman holding child) © Eye Ubiquitous/Tim Page;
(Young girl) © Associated Press/Itsu Inouye
Picture research by Sally Cole

Acknowledgements
Every effort has been made to contact copyright holders of material
reproduced in this book. Any omissions will be rectified in
subsequent printings if notice is given to the publishers.

Barnsley Council for the case study on p. 17 © Reproduced by kind
permission of Barnsley Metropolitan Borough Council; © 'Show
racism the Red card' for the logo on p. 36; © Kick it out
www.kickitout.org for the logo on p. 36; Logo on p. 45 © Refugee
Council. Reproduced by kind permission; © BBC News website
http://news.bbc.co.uk for the case study on p. 46; Logo of
Commission for racial equality on p. 47 © By permission of the
CRE; © The Press Association 2002 for the article on p. 48; © BBC
News website http://news.bbc.co.uk for the case study on p. 53;
Pengiun for the extract from Zlata Filipovic's dairy on p. 55; ©
UNHCR, © Reproduced by kind permission of UNICEF UK, ©
Oxfam logo reproduced with permission of Oxfam publishing, 274
Banbury Road, Oxford OX2 7DZ, for the logos on p. 56; © Greer
Holmes Prison Me! No Way! www.fp.pmnwt.f9.co.uk for the poem
on p. 70; © BBC News website http://news.bbc.co.uk for the article
on p. 72; © Save the Children, © Amnesty International for the
logos on page 85; Everywhere words and music by Gregory B.
Trooper, Sid Griffin © Copyright Universal/Island Music Publishing

(100%) Used by permission of Music Sales. All Rights Reserved.
International Copyright Secured.© The Guardian Angelique
Chrisafis 8/12/01 for the article on p. 90; © The Press Association
2002 for the article on p. 92; © Peace on Earth Written by
Hewson/Evans/Clayton/Mullen Published by Blue Mountain Music
Ltd/Rykomusic Ltd for the lyrics on p. 94

The publishers would like to thank the following for permission to
use photographs:

SR Greenhill/Richard Greenhill (far left), Corbis/Cameron (left
centre), Photo Objects (right centre), Photofusion/David Montford
(far right) p. 6; Vin Mag Archive (top), Eye Ubiquitous/Paul
Thompson (left), Corbis (centre), Photofusion/Steve Eason (right) p.
8; Vin mag Archive p. 9; Photofusion/Edwin Maynard p. 10; Impact
Photos/Simon Shepherd p. 12; Format/Ulrike Preuss p. 13;
Format/Melanie friend (top left), Photofusion/Liam Bailey (bottom
left), Corbis (top right), Corbis (bottom right) p. 14; Barnsley Town
Council (top), John Cole (bottom) p. 17; Eye Ubiquitous/Paul
Seheult (left), S&R Greenhill (right) p. 18; Rentokil (left), Photodisc
(right) p. 19; Getty/Daniel Allan (top), Format/Paula Solloway
(centre), Getty (bottom) p. 20; Format/Joanne O'Brien (top), S&R
Greenhill (centre), Photofusion/Roderick Smith (bottom) p. 21;
Impact photos/Ray Roberts (top), Photofusion/Julia Martin
(bottom) p. 22; Photofusion/David Montford (museum),
Photofusion/Ian Simpson (cinema) Corbis (library) p. 24;
Format/Joanne O'Brien p. 25; Eye Ubiquitous/Matt Wilson (left),
Photofusion/Don Gray (right) p. 26; Corbis p. 27; Corbis p. 28; S&R
Greenhill p. 29; Garrett Nagle p. 30; PA/Rebecca Naden p. 31;
Action Plus/Neil Tingle (top), Action Plus (bottom) p. 32; Action
Plus/Glyn Kirk (top), Empics (bottom) p. 33; PA/Deutsche Press p.
34; PA/Phil noble (top), Action Plus/Neil Tingle (bottom) p. 35;
Photofusion/Paul Doyle (left), Haddon Davies (right),
Photofusion/Christa Stadtler (bottom) p. 37; Popperfoto p. 38;
Format/Brenda Prince (a), John Cole (b), Peter Sanders (c),
AP/Alexander Zemlianichenko (d), Mary Evans (e) p. 39; Mary
Evans (top), AKG (bottom)p. 40; AKG p. 41; Reuters/Chip East p.
42; Harcourt Education/Peter Evans p. 43; Format/Maggie Murray
(left), Rex Features (right) p. 44; Panos/Andrew Testa p. 45; Joel
Chant p. 46; Alamy p. 47; PA p. 48; Format/Jacky Chapman p. 50;
Panos/Giacomo pirozzi (a), Panos/Jan Banning (b), PA/EPA (c),
Panos/Karen Robinson (d) p. 52; Vicky Ntetma/BBC p. 53;
Corbis/Robert Patrick p. 54; PA/Martyn Hayhow p. 55; Alamy (a),
Photofusion/Pete Addis (c), Rex/Sipa Press (d) p. 56; Rex/Don
Cravens/Timepix (topright), S & R Greenhill (top left), Panos/Sean
Sprague (bottom) p. 57; John Cole p. 58; Photodisc (policeman),
Corbis p. 59; Eye Ubiquitous/Paul Segeult p. 63; PA p. 64; PA p. 65;
Mary Evans p. 68; PA/Paul Barker p. 70; PA/EPA (top), Corbis
(bottom) p. 71; Impact Photos/Peter Cavendish (top), Impact
Photos/Peter Cavendish (bottom) p. 72; Rex/David Hartley (left),
PA (right), Harcourt Education/Peter Evans (bottom) p. 74;
Photofusion/David Hartley (bottom), Format (right),
Photofusion/Peter Olive (top), Corbis (bottom) p. 79; Christa
Hook/Linden Artists/Harcourt (women voting), Photofusion/David
Montford (woman), Photofusion/Christa Stadtler (man) p. 81;
Getty (woman), Format/Ulrike Preuss (man), Christa Hook/Linden
Artists/Harcourt (votes for women) p. 82; Popperfoto (left), PA/EPA
(centre), Mary Evans (right) p. 83; PA/Paul Faith p. 84; Corbis p.
85; AP/Nick UT (right) Corbis (left) p. 86; PA/EPA p. 87; Corbis p.
88; AP/Carmen Taylor (top), PA/Epa (bottom) p. 89; S&R Greenhill
(chatting), Format/Karen Robinson (praying), Peter Sanders (meal),
Photodisc (mosque) p. 91; PA/EPA p. 92; Alamy p. 94

There are links to relevant web sites in this book. In order to ensure
that the links are up-to-date, that the links work, and that the sites
are not inadvertently linked to sites that could be considered
offensive, we have made the links available on the Heinemann
website at www.heinemann.co.uk/hotlinks. When you access the
site, the express code is **8036P**

Tel: 01865 888058   www.heinemann.co.uk

Contents

Introduction

What is Citizenship?

'Citizenship Education is education for citizenship, behaving and acting as a citizen, therefore it is not just knowledge of citizenship and civil society. It also implies developing values, skills and understanding.' (Crick Report, 1998)

Citizenship is a new National Curriculum subject for students at Key Stages 3 and 4. The aim of the Citizenship Programme of Study that you will follow is that you will develop the knowledge and skills you will need in the twenty-first century to become an informed, active and responsible member of a local, national and global community. As well as appreciating your own needs, you will appreciate the needs and views of others.

Some schools may have a timetable period for Citizenship, but most students at Key Stage 3 will develop their Citizenship understanding in a range of different ways. This may include tutor time, PSHE work, as a part of other subjects, within organized events such as the School Council, or in voluntary work in school or the local community.

As a part of your Citizenship programme you will be encouraged to participate and work with others, both at school and in the wider community. At the end of Key Stage 3 you will be assessed by your teachers, who will discuss your progress and involvement in the school's Citizenship programme.

Each of the *Citizenship in Action* student books has been designed to help you understand the key ideas. The books use case studies to help you to understand important Citizenship issues. The text is written to encourage you to react and contribute with your own ideas and thoughts. Each chapter includes key words and definitions. You should try to learn these words and use them in the activities you will carry out. Many of the activities can be completed alone or within a group - you could even try them out at home! At the end of each chapter there is a review and reflect section which helps you to pull together the ideas that have been mentioned.

Chapter summaries

Chapter 1 - Local community and democracy

Who exercises power and authority, and how are local decisions made? Through the use of case studies you will gain knowledge and understanding of how local councils and democracy work. How are decisions made that affect your everyday life? How can you make your views and opinions heard? Where does the money come from to pay for local government services?

Chapter 2 - Leisure and sport in the local community

From skateboarding to football clubs, what should be provided for local people? Who should decide this and who should pay for any services or facilities that may be provided? You will examine these issues. Leisure and sport create issues concerning the use of space and the need for such developments to be controlled. What problems might result from the building of a major sporting facility in a built up area? Why are open spaces needed? Why do local councils sometimes have to close facilities, even though they may be very popular? You will also look at the issue of rules and laws in sport. How should rules be made? Is bad behaviour in sport beyond the law? What is meant by the terms 'sportmanship' and 'gamesmanship'? Finally, how do we make sure that sport and leisure include everyone? You will examine how campaigns like *Let's Kick Racism out of Football* make a difference.

Chapter 3 -Human rights

Do you know your rights? You will consider the basic rights that all humans should expect. How are your rights protected by the United Nations, the European Convention and the Human Rights Act? Exploring case studies, you will consider what happens when the rights of others are ignored and how the rights of the individual can be affected by those of others. You will also develop an understanding of certain human rights issues, including the rights of refugees. You will also consider your rights and responsibilities as a child and as a pupil in school.

Chapter 4 - Crime and punishment

What is crime, and who are criminals? Why do people commit crime? You will consider the role of the police in todays modern society. You will explore what the law says about young people, and you will discover your rights within the legal system. How are young people treated differently? Through consideration of case studies you will explore the treatment of juveniles within the criminal justice system. You will look at how courts deal with young people, and what life is like on the inside. You will explore the meaning of the term 'stereotype' and how this can result in people being misjudged.

Chapter 5 - Citizenship and history: voting

Democracy and participation is not just about voting every now and again. How else can you take part? What do you look for in someone standing for election? You will explore how participation can take place in schools and what school councils can achieve.

Chapter 6 - Citizenship and history: world peace

By using case studies involving young people, you will explore recent examples of conflict. You will examine the role of the media in reporting conflict. Was 11 September a major turning point ? Will it have an impact on our lives?

Where do you stand now?

As you work through the chapters in the book and the activities you will take part in, think about the following questions:
- How does democracy and participation work in your local community?
- What are the rights of young people?
- How does conflict occur?
- How can you bring about change?

Chapter 1

Local community and democracy

Learn about...

In this chapter you will learn about local government and how some issues are dealt with on a local rather than a national level.

- What type of services are provided by local government?
- How can people get involved in local issues?
- How do local government departments raise money?
- How is money spent locally?

I work at a leisure complex which has swimming pools, a sports hall, squash courts and a dance studio. I manage the team of people who make sure everything is clean, safe and working properly. I started as a lifeguard and went to work in a swimsuit! Now I wear a business suit instead.

Leisure Centre Manager

I manage parks and nature reserves, footpaths and fishing areas. I work with school groups and volunteers who enjoy studying different species of creepy-crawlies! It's not all fun, though. I get complaints about smelly drains and sometimes I have to deal with people who are angry about having strangers walking on their land.

Countryside Manager

At your service

You have probably heard of someone who 'works for the council', but you may be surprised to discover what kinds of things they do.

When people talk about the 'council', they usually mean the local authority for the area they live in. There are over 400 local authorities in the UK. Whether you live in a small village, a big town, a city or the country, there will be a local authority to provide you with the services you need in your everyday life. Here are some of the people who provide these services.

I make sure that shops don't sell goods like fireworks to underage customers. I also check that places such as petrol stations, pubs and shops are selling their products in the correct measures. If you found something nasty in your burger, you could contact me and I would investigate the problem.

Trading Standards Officer

I work on maintaining the roads, repairing potholes and checking drains. I also work on new road systems, laying kerbstones and pavements and putting on the finishing layers of tarmac. My worst nightmare is drilling through a water or gas pipe, but I haven't done this so far!

Road Worker

Getting technical

Nature reserve an area where natural habitats and animals are protected.

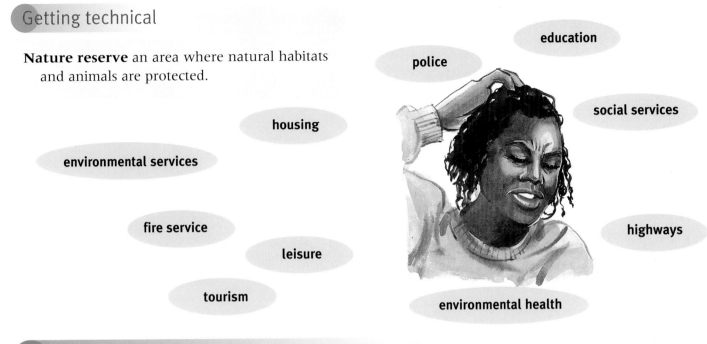

environmental services

housing

fire service

leisure

tourism

police

education

social services

highways

environmental health

Activities

1. In pairs, look at the cartoon above. It lists some of the services your local authority provides. Find the department each council worker belongs to.

2. Imagine you could change places with one of the workers for a day.
   a Which job would you choose?
   b In pairs, discuss why you made your choices and what appeals to you most about the job. What skills might you need to do the work?
   c How does the worker you have chosen provide a service to you or your family?
   d 'You won't believe the day I've had.' In pairs, role-play the conversation you have with a friend when you meet after work. Tell each other about some of the events of the day.

Extension activities

3. Find out about your council's priorities and targets for the next five years. Your council may be able to provide you with this information in a statement of their vision for the future, or a 'Community Strategy'.

4. What impact will the plans have on the lives of you and your family? Discuss what you would like to be included in plans for improvement and share your ideas with the class.

5. Ask a local councillor to visit the school to listen to your ideas for a community policy.

Our Vision of the Future

Providing a safer environment

Keeping our communities clean

Improving facilities for teenagers

The future of our community

It's not natural!

Outrage at discovery of GM crops

Furious residents of Newbridge protested yesterday when they discovered that three fields in the village had been secretly planted with genetically modified (GM) seeds. One resident described the action as 'freakish' and 'like the plot of a science-fiction film'. The residents were worried about long-term health risks and the effects on the food chain.

The crops are part of a three-year trial funded by the government. The aim of the trial is to develop disease-free oilseed rape and beet seeds. There have been rumours of cross-contamination with crops in other fields and the discovery of a new 'superweed' which appeared to be resistant to existing weedkillers.

● *The Newbridge Enquirer*

Lies and cover-ups

Local councillor Moira Davies commented: 'I don't know which is worse. It may be the fact that we have these dangerous experiments with nature on our doorstep, jeopardising the future well being of our children or that the government, which is supposed to be there to help and protect us, does this kind of underhand act behind our backs. I bet the Prime Minister would have something to say if these plants were growing in his garden, but he doesn't care about us.'

There were calls for a public enquiry and a meeting of local residents will take place on Thursday at 6.30pm in the parish hall. All interested parties are welcome to attend.

● The *Day of the Triffids* is a science-fiction novel and film about giant walking plants with deadly stings. They developed as a result of experimentation with plants.

● I protest!

Getting technical

Genetically modified (GM) crops crops that have had their genetic code changed on purpose.

Activities

1. According to the newspaper article, what are the main objections to genetically modified (GM) crops?

2. The article finishes by inviting 'interested parties' to attend a public meeting. Who do you think they have in mind? What might 'interested parties' be concerned about?

Extension activities

3. In small groups, imagine you have been asked to attend the public meeting in Newbridge to represent the views of young people on this issue. Prepare your ideas and discuss the case for and against the development of GM crops. Here are some ideas to start you off, but add to them from your own research.

For	Against
• Disease-free crops means more and better crops to feed the hungry people of the world. • Fewer pesticides and other chemicals used on crops reduces damage to the environment. • Crops which are plentiful bring wealth to communities and provide work for more people.	• 'Superbugs' and 'superweeds' that cannot be controlled may develop as a result of interfering with nature. • Research on rats fed on GM food has shown dangers of damage to the immune system and shortened lifespan, which may also be the effect on humans. • We may destroy forever the naturally growing plants we have now.

4. In your groups, prepare a short presentation using ICT or flip charts. Try to persuade your audience to agree with your point of view.

5. Present your views to the rest of the class, who will act in role as members of the public.

The future

● Poster from the film *Waterworld*

Films and stories which show us a 'nightmare future' are sometimes called 'dystopias'. Often what has caused the dystopia is human interference with nature. Dystopias present the opposite of a perfect world, which is called 'utopia'.

"...SPECTACULAR, EXCITING, EXOTIC."
Tom Charity - TIME OUT
"...ACTION SCENES AND STUNTS THAT WILL TAKE YOUR BREATH AWAY."
Rachael Simpson - DAILY EXPRESS
KEVIN COSTNER
WATERWORLD

"THE BEST EVENT MOVIE OF THE SUMMER"
"A VERY COOL ...CONSTANTLY EXCITING MOVIE"
5 OUT OF 5
★★★★★
MARK WAHLBERG
PLANET OF THE APES
TIM ROTH   HELENA BONHAM CARTER   MICHAEL CLARKE DUNCAN
NOW ODEON
AND AT CINEMAS EVERYWHERE

● Poster from the film *Planet of the Apes*

Activities

1. **a** Can you think of any films, other than those shown above, which present the future of the world as a dystopia?
   b Discuss the events in each film and decide what humans had done to bring about the problems.
   c In each of the films you have thought of, what was the director saying about society?

2. **a** If you were going to write a screenplay which created a future nightmare vision based on the problems in your community, what would be the central idea for your story?
   b Compare your ideas with others in the group.

3. What actions could be taken to prevent current problems affecting the future?

It's all yours!

Imagine a local businesswoman and former pupil of your school has donated this site to your school. The school will use the site as a social club or a mini enterprise centre, where groups of students can raise funds for the school while learning about how to run a business. The businesswoman will donate the money for this and make sure there is proper insurance so that pupils and staff are covered for accidents.

Before any work can start, there are a few problems with the site. Your task is to find out which departments of your local authority can help you sort out these difficulties.

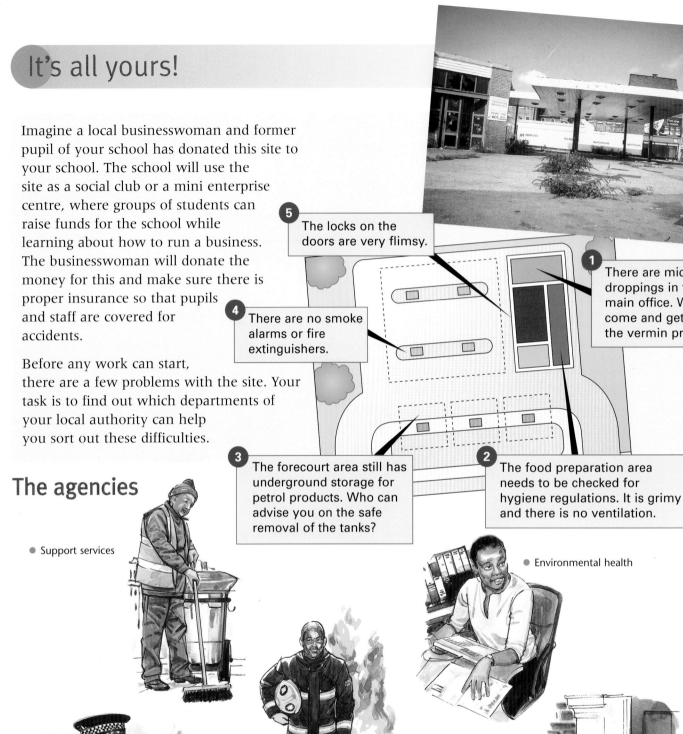

5 The locks on the doors are very flimsy.

1 There are mice droppings in the main office. Who will come and get rid of the vermin problem?

4 There are no smoke alarms or fire extinguishers.

3 The forecourt area still has underground storage for petrol products. Who can advise you on the safe removal of the tanks?

2 The food preparation area needs to be checked for hygiene regulations. It is grimy and there is no ventilation.

The agencies

- Support services

- Environmental health

- The fire service

- The police

- Housing and public health

Activities

1 Which of the five agencies opposite would help you find a solution to the problems with your derelict site?

Can you think of a specialist department within the agency that could provide the service you need?

2 Find out more about the work of the agencies on the Internet by visiting the website for your local council. Find the list of services and take notes about each department and what they deal with. For example, under Support Services you may find:

a Waste management:
- anti-litter campaigns
- refuse and clinical waste collection
- street cleansing
- gully cleansing
- public conveniences (toilets).

b Pest control:
- the dog wardens' service
- 'poopscoop' schemes
- laws about the fouling of footpaths and public areas
- neutering and microchipping schemes
- a laboratory service.

Extension activity

3 What other kinds of problems might you contact your council about? Make a list of ten questions local residents may ask. For each question, draw a picture of the problem or hazard and think of an answer. Look at the example below for ideas.

Q: What happens if my dog goes missing?

A: Your dog may be picked up by the dog warden. A stray dog wearing an identification tag will be returned to its owner, if possible. Dogs found repeatedly straying or dogs without ownership details are taken to RSPCA kennels. The cost of reclaiming a dog from the RSPCA is £65. Stray dogs repeatedly found without identification (collar and ID tag) may cause the owner to be prosecuted.

Enterprise time

Your site problems at the old petrol station have been sorted out, thanks to your local council agencies and your action. Now it is time to think of enterprises you could set up on the site.

Will you be providing a service for the community? For example, you could start up a company called 'Pressed for Time' and do ironing for people. Think of other services you could offer from your site. Could you make the premises into a shop and sell craft items you have made yourself? For example, you could call your shop 'Wick-ed!' and make and sell decorative coloured candles! Or you could turn the premises into a café – you could call it 'In Cod we Trust' and serve fish and chips! Think of some other businesses and catchy company names for them.

wick-ed!
CANDLES

In Cod We Trust

Pressed for Time
—— Ironing service ——

Activities

1. In small groups, share your thoughts and decide which idea would make the most successful business enterprise.

2. Find out if there is a mini enterprise scheme in your school or one run by the local council. This could be a golden opportunity to get involved!

Get the go ahead

Before your new business can get up and running, you may need to find out from your local council about any rules and regulations which could affect your project.

Planning permission is usually needed for building. The planning system is there to make sure that our environment is protected and improved. Planning controls many things including redevelopments and where there are changes in the use of buildings such as shops and restaurants. It even controls tree pruning. You can find out whether you need planning permission by contacting the council and getting pre-application advice. This will help you decide whether your application is likely to be successful or not.

By law, the council has to publicise all planning permission applications. It will write to occupiers of neighbouring properties, or put up a public notice at the site. In many cases, it also writes to residents' or tenants' associations to let them know that an application has been made. Up to 21 days will be allowed for replies and comments. Local people might be worried about litter, parking or noise, for example.

Remember that if you build something which needs planning permission and you do not get this permission beforehand, you might have to knock it down!

Activity

1 Be a planning expert! Decide whether or not the following projects need planning permission. Alongside each project, write DON'T BUILD! if you think permission is needed. Write BUILD! if you think permission is not needed. The answers are provided, but see if you can guess each one before looking at these.

1 Putting up a wall inside your house.
2 Using part of your home for business purposes.
3 Adding a porch to your house.
4 Building a swimming pool in the garden.
5 Building an extension to a factory which is below the height of the building.
6 Adding an extension to your premises which reduces parking space.
7 Changing the use of your premises from a restaurant to a shop.
8 Changing the use of your premises, which means that more people will visit as a result.
9 Starting a business that will cause smells in the neighbourhood.
10 Connecting telephone cables to the outside of your building.

● Your research has paid off. Your premises are ready and you have stuck to the correct regulations. Everything is up and running, ready to go!

Answers
1 BUILD! 2 DON'T BUILD! 3 DON'T BUILD! 4 BUILD! (as long as you do not put a roof on top of it) 5 BUILD! 6 DON'T BUILD! 7 BUILD! 8 DON'T BUILD! 9 DON'T BUILD! 10 BUILD!

Spend, spend, spend!

The local council has to provide many services to the public. All these services cost money. Over £60 billion is spent by local councils every year in England alone.

Where does the money go?

Some of the money is passed straight to the police and fire services. Most of the rest of the money goes on education and social services. What is left is spent on environmental services, such as street cleaning and refuse collection, as well as tourism and culture, planning and housing.

Where does the money come from?

Most of the money the council receives comes from the government. The rest comes from council tax, which is paid by householders. The amount they pay depends on where they live and the size and value of their home.

● The government   ● Town Hall   ● Tax payers

Who decides on how much to spend and what to spend it on?

Local councillors are elected by local people in local elections. People stand for election. They usually belong to a political party whose members share a vision of how they would like society to be and what things should be done to make this happen. The elected councillors meet and decide how any available money should be spent. Each party has its own priorities. One party may favour spending more on environmental projects while another may be keen to improve education.

Activities

The money your local council receives has been distributed to the different departments, but there is £500,000 still to be handed out. The political parties will decide which departments to favour.

1
  a In small groups, form your own political party. Choose a name for your party and decide on what kind of services you would like to support with the extra money.
  b Look at the list below, and decide how you would share out the £500,000 between the departments. Be ready to say why you made your choices by saying why the departments you favour are valuable to your community.
  c Discuss your ideas with the rest of the class.

A Trading Standards Department
- Animal Health and Welfare Section
- Extra amount requested: £350,000
- We visit farms and abattoirs and check on the health of livestock. We are committed to safeguarding the welfare of the animals and want to make sure there is no danger to humans through the spread of disease.

B Social Services
- Social Work Section
- Extra amount requested: £200,000
- We deal with all kinds of family support cases. Sometimes we help children when they are having problems at home because of illness in the family or domestic violence.

C Education
- Curriculum Support Section
- Extra amount requested: £65,000
- We provide support for people of all ages and abilities. For example, we provide classroom support assistants who help pupils with special needs.

D Corporate Services
- Human Resources Section
- Extra amount requested: £275,000
- Every council has 'core' or corporate services which plan and implement its work. Covering personnel, information technology, marketing and legal matters, we make sure everything runs properly and that the community gets the services they need.

E Leisure Services
- Museums and Galleries Section
- Extra amount requested: £50,000
- We have the possibility of a major new exhibition of local art which will provide a showcase for our community talent. We need people to organize the venues, order transport and design the plan for the exhibits; lighting, labelling and marketing.

F Tourism Department
- Extra amount requested: £25,000
- We promote local attractions and organize events that bring visitors into the area. These events also make the place fun to live in for local residents. Visitors spend money and create opportunities for new jobs, so improving the area for all of us.

G The Police Force
- Extra amount requested: £85,000
- We want to set up a special section to help reduce and prevent cases of 'hate crime' and to work positively with young people to reduce offending. We need funds for training our officers.

Extension activity

2 Invite your council's finance officer to come and speak to you about how your council decides to spend its money.

Making local democracy fun!

Local authorities are keen to involve citizens in the work that they do. Read the extract below from Barnsley Local Council's website. Go to www.heinemann.co.uk/hotlinks and click on this activity for more information about Barnsley's Local Council.

Case study 1: Local Democracy Week 2002

The Local Government Association's (LGA) Local Democracy Week is now entering its fifth year. With around 300 local authorities taking part annually the week is proving to be an extremely successful national event.

In 2001 a Barnsley Town Hall Open Day gave people an opportunity to visit the council's most prestigious building. This allowed them to see displays providing information about council services and also the historic silver collection and the Council Chamber. It also gave them a rare opportunity to climb to the top of the town hall tower to view the surrounding countryside.

A variety of vehicles, provided by the council and the fire service, were parked on the concourse and entertainment was provided by local musicians and dancers. There was a quiz and colouring competition for young people and one lucky visitor won a computer and software package – just for turning up!

The event this year will take place nationally in October.

Activity

1. Plan an event for Local Democracy Week, using ideas from the article above and some of your own. In groups, timetable a series of events for your school and local community. Present your ideas in a display using your artistic and ICT skills.

    Include:

    - departments and services from the local council
    - activities for children and adults
    - ideas for street theatre (for example, living statues, mime, juggling), perhaps with a theme taken from events in local history
    - tours, drama, sports.

What is community?

Think about the word 'community'. What does it mean to you? You can belong to several communities: your school community, the neighbourhood community, a sport and leisure community.

A community is not just made up of the people who live in a particular place. It includes the buildings that people use, the services people have access to, and the way people feel and behave.

Activities

1. Make a list of all the things that you feel your community includes.

2. Explain why each item on your list is part of your community.

   a Think about the things in your community that make you feel happy and proud. Draw a spider diagram or mind map to explain your choices. You could use the one below to start you off.

because I enjoy playing in the park with my friends

My community makes me happy and proud

   b Think about the things in your community that make you feel sad and angry. Draw a spider diagram or mind map to explain your choices.

   c For each entry in your 'sad and angry' mind map, make one suggestion about how the situation could be improved. Remember that the situation should be improved for everyone in your community, not just you.

Fiesta time in Soaptown

Activities

You have been asked to attend a storyline conference for a new daily drama programme to be screened on TV. The title for the show is *Soaptown*, but you will be able to suggest a more interesting name. In the first three episodes in the drama, the characters get involved in the community Local Democracy Week. You have to decide what happens to each of them and describe the events that will make exciting viewing in the all-important first episodes. For example an event could involve PH setting up a practical joke at the launch of Local Democracy week. The joke goes wrong but luckily NG manages to save the day. NG could be very annoyed that the event was nearly ruined by PH's pranks.

1. The pictures show some of the characters, who are identified by their initials only. You have to come up with the names!

2. Hold your storyline conference and get those episodes moving! Present your ideas in either script or story form.

Extension activity

3. Ask your teacher if you can act out part of an episode and record it using a video or digital camera.

PH: Works in the Pest Control department. Is a bit of a practical joker and sometimes upsets people, but never means any real harm.

PG: Pupil in the local secondary school. Not very happy at the moment - experiencing problems at home. Needs someone to confide in. He puts a brave face on things and tries to keep cheerful.

NG: Firefighter and all-round cool guy. Very keen to help children understand the dangers of fire. Intends to run workshops for Events Week. Is more frightened of speaking in public than of fighting fires.

CS: Manager in charge of the day nursery. Always in and out of love. Bit of a chocoholic, loves dangerous stunts.

NL: Former resident of Soaptown, now a celebrity who is coming back to officially open the event. Lots of publicity about the visit in the local press.

Review and reflect

Local authorities want more people to be aware of the work they do. They also want local people to participate, where possible.

Case study 2: Swansea's youth services

Swansea's young at heart

The council of Swansea has developed a reputation for listening to its young people. Swansea Council sets out to involve young people in decisions about their local services and issues that matter to them. They do this through regular working groups where young people meet with councillors and staff, and an annual youth conference attended by up to 200 young people.

Several local projects have been set up, including a youth information centre and a

Children and Young People's Charter, which promotes young people's interests to local businesses, public services and the media.

Vivienne Sugar, Chief Executive of the City and County of Swansea says: 'I am delighted that the work of councillors, officers and of young people themselves is being recognized. Local government must respond to young people's needs.'

● At the heart of Swansea

Activities

1. What advantages would there be if more young people participated in local affairs:
   a to young people
   b to the council?

2. What kind of projects would you like to be involved with in your community?

3. Taking part in the life of the community is an important part of being a citizen. It can also be fun. How would you encourage other people to participate in the local community?

Chapter 2

Leisure and sport in the local community

Learn about...

In the first chapter you learned about how we are governed locally and how local issues are dealt with. In this chapter we will look at how sport and leisure facilities are provided for local communities, by looking at the questions below.

- What do the words 'leisure' and 'sport' mean?
- Where does the money come from to pay for leisure and sport facilities?
- How does the council decide its priorities when spending money?
- Why is planning important and what issues does it create?
- Why do most sports and leisure activities need to have rules and why are officials important?
- Why is it important that everyone is included in plans about which leisure and sport facilities are set up?

Think about the things you like to do in your free time. Think about the activities and sports you and your friends take part in. Imagine your life without these activities. How important are these activities to you and your friends?

Getting technical

Sport and leisure facilities places where local people can go to play and watch sport, or places like libraries, parks and museums.

● This is a leisure centre, which has been built by the local council for the community

● Sometimes local councils run out of money and cannot afford to keep facilities open

Leisure and sport in the local community

We sometimes take for granted the range of local sports and leisure facilities that we use. They may have been there for a long time, but who provides them and who pays for them?

Many of these facilities are provided by local councils. They are just a small part of all the things needed by people in local communities. They are paid for from the money raised by the council from council tax. They may also be paid for by grants made by the government or by other sources like the National Lottery fund.

What is a local council?

A local council is a group of people who are elected by their own community every four years in local elections. Any adult may stand for election as a local councillor. Councillors are responsible for the provision of local services and the money needed to provide them.

The workings of a local council is often called local government. This is different to the national government in Westminster, where Parliament sits. Parliament gives local government the power to run local services.

● This is the national government in Westminster

● These people belong to a local government. Local government means the council in your area

What do the words 'sport' and 'leisure' mean?

These words are often linked with physical activities like rugby, soccer and swimming. While this is often true, many leisure activities do not involve much physical activity at all. For example, reading, visiting a theatre or a museum, and watching a movie at the cinema are all leisure activities that many people enjoy.

People choose to spend their free time in different ways. Most local councils think it is important to provide for a wide range of interests. Some of these activities, like cinemas and theatres, are paid for by private companies. Others, like libraries and museums, are paid for by the local council.

In many areas, local parks meet a wide range of leisure-time needs, with their quiet walks and flowers in one area and sports pitches and children's playground elsewhere.

So, all free-time activities may be called leisure activities, but not all of them involve sport.

● Local museums, libraries and art galleries are usually paid for by the local council

Activities

1. List all the leisure facilities provided by the local council in your area. Compare your list with other people in your class.

2. Create a master list of all the facilities provided in your area. Copy and complete a large table like the one below. Write details from your master list in the right places.

The facilities that are for sport	The facilities that are not for sport

● Cinemas are usually paid for by private companies

3. a How would the use of a local swimming pool be different for older people, family groups or competitive swimmers?
   b How are the needs of different groups catered for in your local area?

Extension activity

4. Find out about sports and leisure facilities in your area. Visit these facilities and try to find out as much as you can about these places. Use the questions below to start off your research. You could then think of other things you might like to find out.
   a When was your local park first opened?
   b How has its use changed since then?
   c Who controls how the park is laid out and decides what activities are provided for the community?
   d When was your local swimming pool opened?
   e Why do some older swimming pools have the words 'public baths' over the main entrance?
   f Who paid for these older swimming pools when they were first opened?

How does the local council pay for leisure and sport?

Where does the money come from?

Your local council receives money (revenue) from several sources:

- local householders, shops and businesses that pay council tax
- government grants to help with funding some major projects
- money raised from some of the services it offers, such as swimming pools, tennis courts in local parks, hiring sports pitches and facilities at sports centres, and car parks.

The council makes a list each year of everything it needs to spend money on. Any money the council intends to spend on leisure or sports facilities is agreed at council meetings. Councillors must discuss any objections and cut down their list of projects to the ones the council can afford.

Leisure and sport are not the only services that the council must provide. This can mean that some projects have to be postponed until a later time or cancelled altogether. It can also mean that some existing facilities may have to be closed down.

Which facilities should the local council provide?

The council has some difficult decisions to make. It would be impossible to provide for every sports and leisure activity.

● Swimming pools bring in a lot of money but not nearly enough to cover the amount it costs to run them

When they decide which activities or facilities to support, councils think about a number of issues:

- the cost of providing and maintaining each facility
- the number of people who might use each facility
- the effects of each facility on the local area, for example, noise, traffic, safety or inconvenience to non-users
- whether it is acceptable to provide some activities that may only appeal to a small number of people, for example skateboarding parks
- the need to provide facilities for:
  - very young children
  - older people
  - disability groups
  - ethnic minority groups.

Decisions, decisions

Some amenities, like swimming pools, are very expensive to run, but lots of people want to use them. Others may be used by many different people and appeal to a whole range of interests (for example, public parks). Local councils must decide what facilities they can afford to build and operate. They may also have to make decisions about which facilities should be closed down and when this should happen. Their decisions may be based on some of the considerations listed on the previous page.

● Local councils have to decide which facilities they can afford to run

Activities

1 Imagine your local council must decide whether to close down the bowling green or the skateboarding area in your local park. Although the council would like to continue to keep both going, there is not enough money to do this. The chairperson of the Amenities Committee has called a meeting at which a decision must be made.

  a The class should be divided into two groups of councillors who will be on opposite sides of the argument.

  b Vote for someone from your class to act as the chairperson.

  c Vote for one person from each group of councillors to speak for each side.

  d Vote for another person from each group to support the leading speakers.

  e The chairperson will then run a debate on the issue. Your teacher will tell you about the rules on how to hold a debate.

  f The debate should include reasons for supporting and opposing each activity.

  g At the end of the debate, voting should take place, with each councillor raising his or her hand in support of their preferred activity.

2 **a** Imagine that you use the facility that the council has decided to close. Organize a petition to present to the Amenities Committee at its next meeting, asking it to think again about its decision.

  b Design a poster and plan a leaflet campaign in your area to gain support for your petition.

  c Can you think of any other ways in which you might persuade the Amenities Committee to change its mind?

Hold a debate

After you have elected your spokesperson and supporter, discuss your views in small groups.

- Make sure you hear everyone's point of view if they have one.
- Make sure no one is put down or ignored.
- Try to back up what you say with evidence rather than just your views.

Which facilities would you keep open?

Swimming pools are one of the most expensive facilities to build and maintain, so why do local councils close them only as a very last resort?

Think about the consequences of closing a swimming pool. Where would people learn to swim in safety? Although keeping a swimming pool open might be expensive, local councils usually do everything they can to keep them open. This might mean that something else has to be closed down to save money.

Other tough decisions

Remember that local councils cannot provide for every leisure or sports activity. There may be people in your community who like doing something that not many people enjoy. They may feel that they should have a facility for them to use. There may be other people who are interested in activities that are very expensive to run.

If the council pays for these facilities out of their limited pot of money, it would then have to reduce the number of more popular activities that it could provide.

Can you think of any examples of facilities that it would be unrealistic to expect your local council to provide?

Campaign an organized course of action to get the public's support for something.
Consequences the effects of something.

Planning for leisure and sport

As well as costing money, both leisure and sport use something else that is valuable – space!

This is a very important thing to think about, especially in built-up areas. In those places, the space is needed for shops, businesses, houses and public buildings, as well as areas for leisure and sports activities.

All the above uses of space involve the whole community. The local council's planning committee can grant or refuse permission to build or develop in the area.

Many towns have grown up over hundreds of years and the need for recreational space was not always considered to be as important as it is today.

The council must consider two issues:

- Changing how an area of land is used. This is often called redevelopment.
- Allowing land, which has never been built on, to be used for new development. This new development may be for leisure or sport, but it may also be for new houses, shops or to build new factories or businesses.

In both the issues there are building regulations that control what can be built and where. These regulations apply just as much to leisure and sport facilities as they do to any other development.

Getting technical

Recreational space space that is used by people in their spare time.
Building regulations rules covering how, where and what can be built.
'Greenbelt' land land around the outskirts of towns that has never been built on.

Considerations

When a planning application is made, the local council must make sure that three points have been met:

- that the building or development will be safe and that it will be built in line with current building regulations
- that any social or environmental issues have been thought about. These might include:
  - the use of 'greenbelt' land – land that has never been built upon
  - noise or other hazards to people living nearby or people using the facility
  - traffic problems that might be caused by the planned development
- that anyone who wants to object to the proposed development is given the chance to do this.

● Traffic, transport and environmental issues need to be thought about carefully

Activities

Imagine your local football club has plans to redevelop its old stadium so it can meet modern safety regulations and fit more people in.

The club has sent the following draft proposals to the local council for them to consider:

Proposal A: To redevelop the old stadium on its present site near the town centre. This means buying some old and derelict properties nearby, knocking the buildings down and using the land as part of the new stadium and as an extra car park.

Proposal B: To build a brand new stadium on a 'greenbelt' site on the outskirts of the town. The sale of the old stadium for housing land will bring in the money for this.

1 What problems might be caused by each proposal? Think about the people who live near to the old stadium and the new site.

2 What other groups of people might be affected by the proposals? Think about local shops and businesses, and the people who provide transport and emergency services.

3 What part would the local council play in each proposed development?

4 How would all the people affected be given a chance to have their say?

Case study 1: Oxford United

● The old stadium at Manor Ground

In 1995 Oxford United football club said they would be leaving their stadium at Manor Ground, Headington because it was not big enough for a modern club and could seat only 10,000 fans. It was built in a housing area that was hard for fans to get to, with limited parking and few facilities inside the ground.

Local residents were against the move. They thought the football ground brought more advantages than disadvantages to the area. Fans spent money in the shops and pubs close to the stadium, which was good for the area but not for the football club.

In 1996 the club started to build a new stadium on a larger site at Minchery Farm. As well as the football pitch, this site includes a hotel, a conference centre, a cinema, a gym and a bowling alley. These facilities can be used throughout the year, not just on match days. There are enough parking spaces for 2000 cars and 15 coaches. There are no other facilities nearby, which means fans spend more money inside the stadium. There is also plenty of room around the site to expand and develop new facilities.

● Minchery Farm, the new site

Regulating leisure and sport

For most people, leisure activities are meant to be enjoyable. Even most professional sportspeople say that being able to enjoy their sport is just as important as the money they earn from being good at it.

However, even in sport there are always people whose behaviour is unacceptable. So that other people are not harmed by this behaviour, leisure and sporting activities need to take place within certain guidelines. This is to make them as safe as possible, and to make sure that everyone gets a fair chance.

- Although leisure and sport are a small part of everyday life, the country's laws still apply to them.
- The rules laid down by sports governing bodies should make it clear what is unacceptable behaviour. They should say how unacceptable behaviour should be dealt with.
- Leisure and sporting activities should not exclude ethnic and other minority groups.

For many years, bad tackling or physical assault during play were seen as 'just part of the game'. This is no longer the case and sportspeople who do this are punished. The punishment might be a fine or suspension. This is decided by the governing body of their sport.

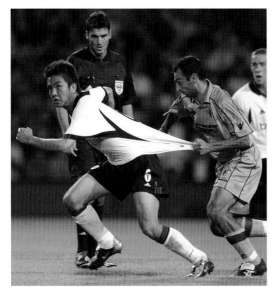

● Is this acceptable?

It is not just players who can be punished. People in charge of leisure activity groups who do not carry out their responsibilities properly may also be punished.

Pressure like this can often tempt sportspeople (and sometimes coaches and officials) to 'stretch' the rules or cheat. Does this make cheating acceptable?

Getting technical

Professional sportsmen and women who earn their living from sport.
Governing bodies the organizations responsible for each sport.
Suspension when someone is not allowed to take part in an activity for a period of time.
Amateurs sportspeople who are not paid.
Sponsorship when a person or company offers money in return for advertising.

What has changed?

In many sports, the days when most people at the top level were amateurs are now gone. In many professional sports, the money people earn in a year is well beyond what most ordinary people can hope to earn in a lifetime.

Sponsorship involving large sums of money has also created pressure on sportsmen and women (and their clubs) to win. Sponsors do not like to be associated with failure!

Official responsibility

Sporting activities take place within a set of rules, and players have a responsibility to be aware of these rules.

But what about the officials? How far is it up to them to make sure the rules are not ignored?

Why are officials needed?

Many decisions in sport need to be made by an unbiased official. It would be very difficult for sportspeople to make decisions when all their thoughts are focused on their performance. In a close sprint finish it would be impossible for the athletes to decide who finished first, second and third.

Many people believe that in order to enable referees and other officials to do the job properly, they should be paid a professional salary. This would allow them to become as good at their job as the players they take charge of.

Some referees in soccer and umpires in cricket, for example, have been criticized since the use of instant video replays. In many cases, their decisions have been shown to be wrong.

Unbiased without supporting one side or the other.
Salary a yearly wage.

● Officials are needed to make sure players behave properly

● Officials are not paid nearly as much as the sportspeople themselves

Playing to the rules

It is becoming common to hear of players 'bending' the rules or breaking them if they think they can get away with it.

In some sports, an aggressive attitude towards the opposition can go too far. Some players mean to harm the opposition as part of their game. Outside of sport, people who act like this would find themselves in serious trouble. For example, if two people started a fight in the street, it is likely that they would be arrested and charged with assault.

There is really no difference between this type of incident and one that just happens to take place in a premier league football match or on the local playing fields on a Sunday morning.

Cheating

Cheating can take many forms, and often what some people think is cheating others think is not. Look at the photograph to the right. This is the famous 'hand of God' incident involving Argentina's Diego Maradona. In 1986, England played Argentina in a World Cup game. Maradona scored a goal which the England team claimed was a hand-ball goal. Argentina won 2-1.

It became clear from video replays that the England team were right. Maradona had indeed guided the ball into the net with his hand.

It is difficult to say whether actions like this are premeditated or whether they occur on the spur of the moment. In either case, it is still cheating.

Getting technical

Premeditated planned in advance.
Beta blockers drugs that slow the heart down and calm the nerves.
Performance-enhancing drugs drugs taken to improve a player's game.

● It is not acceptable to fight on the sports field

● Maradona helped Argentina win against England with this hand ball

Activities

1 **a** What different ways of cheating in sport can you think of?

   b What should happen to the player who cheats in each case?

2 How would you use modern technology to try to make sure that cheating was kept to a minimum?

3 Discussion: Will levels of cheating rise as the money people can earn in sport rises?

Extension activities

4 Imagine a leading sportswoman has been found guilty of taking beta blockers for non-medical reasons. This is the second time this has happened and she is banned for life by her sports governing body.

   a Hold a class discussion about whether or not this punishment is unreasonable.

   b Is it against the law to take beta blockers outside sport?

   c If you were the sportswoman and her manager, what things would you do in the light of this ban?

5 Hold a class debate to discuss the following statement: 'A sports performer who takes drugs for genuine medical reasons – but who still competes – is less of a cheat than the performer who has no medical reasons to take drugs.'

6 As a class, copy and complete a large table like the one below. List the reasons why taking performance-enhancing drugs should be banned or allowed.

Reasons why drugs should be banned	Reasons why drugs should be allowed

7 Some sporting authorities take the serious step of banning for life those people found guilty of more than one offence. Many first offenders are banned for up to four years, which is almost half a career in sporting terms.

The best-known example of this is possibly Ben Johnson, the sprinter who was banned for life after testing positive for drugs at the Olympics in Seoul in 1988.

Johnson later had his lifetime ban overturned but by then it was too late to resume his career as a top international sprinter.

   a Use the list of different ways of cheating you drew up in Activity 1 and put them in order of seriousness.

   b How do you think each type of offence should be punished? Does each punishment match the seriousness of the offence?

● Ben Johnson was banned for life when he used drugs to help his performance

Including everyone

Modern sport should include everyone. Local council policies for leisure and sport should pay attention to the needs of all groups, including:

- very young children
- older people
- disability groups
- ethnic minority groups
- women's groups
- disadvantaged groups (for example, people living in poor, inner-city areas and those living in remote rural areas).

Sport is not only for young people. The current World Veterans' record for the 100 metres sprint for 55-year-olds is 11.39 seconds for men and 13.43 sec for women. How many of us can run that fast?

The Commonwealth Games in Manchester also showed the world that people with disabilities can be world-class athletes.

In recent years, opportunities in sport have also increased for ethnic minorities in the UK. The mix of people at the top levels of sport is slowly beginning to include people of all races and backgrounds.

Activities

1. Investigate the ways in which your local council provides for the groups listed at the top of the page. Are all these groups provided for? If not, see if you can find out why.

2. Are there sports clubs for people with disabilities in your area? Which sports are catered for and who provides the facilities?

3. Do you know anyone older, perhaps older family members, who still take part in sport? Ask them about the facilities they use and who provides them.

Changing minds

In the past twenty years, more attention has been paid to the breaking down of old prejudices and barriers in sport. This has given more people the chance to take part in leisure and sports activities.

Local and national governments, as well as sporting organizations, encourage policies of 'inclusiveness' by promoting or supporting campaigns. These campaigns might be to get rid of violence and racism in sport, or to encourage more people from minority groups to take part in sport.

In addition, many local and national sports facilities are now designed with facilities for disabled groups.

Some sporting and leisure activities have traditionally been seen as 'male' or 'female'. Think about rugby, netball, snooker and hockey – how do you picture the players? Gradually, however, this is beginning to change. People are realizing that all sports are for everyone.

How many sports teams are there for boys and for girls in your school? If they are unequal in number, why do you think this is?

Activities

There are two main campaigns against racism in sport:

Show Racism the Red Card.

Let's Kick Racism out of Football

1 Go to www.heinemann.co.uk/hotlinks and click on the websites of these campaigns. Read through them to get an idea of how the campaigns are put together.

2 Choose one of the following groups:
  • disability groups
  • local pensioners
  • the long-term unemployed.

a Plan a campaign to improve access to leisure and sport for your chosen group. Your campaign should consist of a poster to display in public and a leaflet to explain the details of the campaign. You can assume that your campaign has the backing of the local council, with its facilities at your disposal.

b Where would you display your posters? Where and how would you give out your leaflets?

Review and reflect

In this chapter you have learned that although your local council provides a wide range of leisure and sport facilities, this is not done without some difficulty.

One of the lessons you have learned from working through this chapter is that we must be prepared to consider the needs of others as well as our own needs.

There are two other lessons in this chapter. First, life in any community depends on people valuing what is provided for them and using these facilities in a way that will not cause problems for other people. Second, no group of individuals is more important than another. We should not expect that expensive leisure facilities should be provided for one small group of people at the expense of other groups in the community.

Activities

1 Look back at the issues you have studied in this chapter. Decide which are the three most important issues for:

a planning which sports and leisure facilities to provide.

b making rules and regulations in sport.

c making sure sport and leisure includes everyone.

2 a List all the positive effects that sport and leisure facilities bring to the local community.

b List any negative effects of sport and leisure facilities you can think of.

c On balance, do you think that sports and leisure facilities are good for local communities?

Chapter 3

Human rights

Learn about...

In this chapter you will think about how important it is to respect other people's human rights and what happens when rights are not respected.

- What are the basic human rights?
- How have human rights developed through the years in the UK and around the world?
- What are the rights of children in school and across the world?
- What happens when human rights are ignored?
- How can the rights of the individual and of society be different?
- Which agencies support and uphold human rights?
- Do rights come with responsibilities?

● The rights of others have not always been respected

Activities

1. Your class needs to set some ground rules for discussion. Look at this classroom cartoon. Discuss with a partner what the pupils are doing that shows they are not having a good discussion.

2. Share your ideas with the rest of the class.

3. Copy the following rules for good listening. Add to it any extra rules of your own.

   - Listen to what other pupils have to say.
   - Look at the person who is speaking.
   - Be prepared to add your own ideas.
   - Be prepared to change your ideas.
   - Do not distract other pupils.
   - Do not make fun of what other pupils say.
   - Do not shout out.

What are human rights?

Activity

1. Imagine you are an alien who has landed on earth. Write a report for your leaders back home about the humans you find on earth. Tell them what humans look like and what they need to stay alive. Then tell your leaders what else humans need to be happy, healthy and fulfilled.

There are certain basic rights and freedoms to which all people are entitled. However, it has taken a long time for these human rights to be agreed and written down.

During the twentieth century these rights were set out to include:

- equality of treatment
- freedom of speech
- tolerance of other people's beliefs
- respect for the ideas of others.

Some countries, though, have treated people badly and have taken away their rights.

Getting technical

Equality having the same rights.
Freedom having no restrictions placed on you.
Respect consideration towards another person.
Tolerance willingness to allow people to live as they like, even if they are different from you.

A

B

C

D

E

1. Look at pictures A, B and C on page 39. Describe what is happening in each picture. Which human right does each image represent?

2. Look at pictures D and E. Describe what is happening in each picture. How are human rights being affected in each image? How do you think the people affected feel?

Extension activity

3. Use the Internet to find out how the South African government in the twentieth century denied the human rights of certain groups of people. Write a newspaper article on your findings.

What human rights did the people of Nazi Germany have?

After coming to power in Germany on 30 January 1933, the Nazi Party, led by Adolf Hitler, started an anti-Semitism campaign against Jews. Their businesses were destroyed, they had their German citizenship taken away, they were banned from voting and were not allowed to marry non-Jews.

Many Jews were sent to concentration camps. These camps would hold people who were arrested for no reason. People were beaten, starved and made to work. Some had terrible medical experiments carried out on them. By 1939 about 25,000 prisoners (mainly Jews, but also communists, socialists and Jehovah's Witnesses) were held in concentration camps.

In 1942 the Nazis organized the Final Solution - the mass extermination of Jews by gassing rather than shooting. The Nazis set up death camps, such as Auschwitz and Bergen-Belsen, where entire populations were killed. In these camps, millions of Jews were gassed and their bodies burnt.

In total during the Holocaust, over 6 million people were killed. Most of them were Jews. To help the Nazis achieve this, they carried out a propaganda campaign against Jews. The German people were told that Jews were bad for Germany. They said that Jews were to blame for unemployment and high prices, as well as all the other problems faced by the German people at that time.

● Jews were made to wear a badge to show they were Jewish

● Many thousands of people were murdered in death camps like Auschwitz

Getting technical

Anti-Semitism hatred of Jews.

Holocaust the programme of hatred and mass murder of Jews by the Nazis before and during the Second World War.

Propaganda organized programme of information used to spread beliefs.

Campaign an organized course of action to get the public's support for something.

Case study 1: Anne Frank's diary

Anne Frank was born on 12 June 1929 in Frankfurt, Germany. In 1933 the anti-Jewish Nazi Party came to power. Anne's Jewish parents decided to take the family to the safety of the Netherlands, where they lived a normal life until 1940. But in 1940 Germany invaded the Netherlands, and life for the Franks became more difficult. So, in 1942, the family, together with four other people, went into hiding in an annex of rooms above Anne's father's office in Amsterdam.

While she was in hiding, Anne and the others had to keep quiet and not move about during the day in case they were heard by the Nazi Secret Police. To relieve her boredom, one of the things Anne did during the next two years was to write a diary.

Mostly, people keep diaries to write down private thoughts. Anne tried to write about daily life in the annex and the news from the outside world too. Sometimes there were exciting things to report, such as a bombing or a break-in in the middle of the night. Anne describes the ups and downs of those living in hiding in an honest way.

Eventually, however, the Nazis discovered their hiding place. Anne, her family, and the others living with them were arrested and sent to concentration camps. In March 1945, nine months after she was captured, Anne Frank died of typhus at Bergen-Belsen concentration camp. She was 15 years old.

Her diary, which filled several notebooks, was published in 1947. It has since been translated into more than 60 languages and *The Diary of Anne Frank* has become one of the most popular books in the world.

Activities

1. The Nazis forced Jews to wear a yellow star on their clothes. What else did the Nazis do to them? How did this affect their human rights?

2. Why did the German people accept what was happening to the Jews?

3. Imagine you are a Jew living in Nazi Germany during the Second World War. Write a letter to a friend in the UK explaining what life is like for you.

4. Read the case study about Anne Frank. Discuss with a partner how her human rights were affected by the Nazis. Then discuss your ideas with the rest of the class.

Extension activities

5. Write a diary entry for one day in Anne Frank's life in hiding.

How to...
Write a diary
- You need to start your diary with the day and the date.
- The things you write about should be written in the order in which they happened during the day.
- For each of the things you write about, give an idea of the time of day, for example, before breakfast.

6. Some Jewish people prefer to use another word for the terrible things the Nazis did to Jews in the 1930s and 1940s. Go to www.heinemann.co.uk/hotlinks and use the 'About the Holocaust' section of the Yad Vashem website to try to find out what word they prefer and why.

Human rights legislation

The United Nations takes action to protect human rights

After the Second World War, the United Nations (UN) was set up to try to resolve conflict without war. The UN states that one of its main purposes is 'to encourage respect for human rights and for basic freedoms for all'.

On 10 December 1948 the UN set out the Universal Declaration of Human Rights. This stated that all member countries of the UN had to protect certain rights, including the right to life, liberty and freedom of speech. The UN also set up a department which is responsible for monitoring human rights around the world.

The Universal Declaration of Human Rights formed the basis for more than 80 other declarations on human rights, including some on the rights of children.

Here is an extract from the Universal Declaration of Human Rights. There are 30 Articles in total.

● The United Nations Headquarters in New York

UNIVERSAL DECLARATION OF HUMAN RIGHTS

THIS UNIVERSAL DECLARATION OF HUMAN RIGHTS is a common standard of achievement for all peoples and all nations.

Article 1
You have the same human rights as everyone else in the world, because you are a human being. These rights cannot be taken away from you. Everybody, no matter who they are or where they live, should be treated with dignity.

Article 2
You should not be treated differently, nor have your rights taken away, because of your race, colour, sex, language, religion or political opinions. Your basic rights should be respected no matter what country you are born in or how rich or poor you are.

The European Convention on Human Rights

After the UN had set down its Universal Declaration of Human Rights, the Council of Europe decided to create a set of human rights for the people of Europe. On 4 November 1950 representatives from the European countries signed the European Convention on Human Rights. The UK was one of the first countries to accept the convention when it was passed through Parliament in 1951.

Three organizations were also set up to make sure the convention is followed:

- The European Commission of Human Rights
- The European Court of Human Rights
- The Committee of Ministers of the Council of Europe.

These organizations allow people to challenge how they are treated in their own country. A person's case is heard by a panel of judges in the European Court of Human Rights. Once a country has accepted the convention, the European Court's decision is final.

The Human Rights Act 1998

The UK accepted the European Convention on Human Rights in 1951. However, it was not until 1966 that people were given the right to take a case to the European Court of Human Rights in Strasbourg, France. Things changed again in 1998 when the Human Rights Act was introduced. This made the rights set out in the European Convention on Human Rights part of British law. This has made it much easier and quicker for British people to follow up human rights issues, as cases are now tried in courts in Britain. After being heard in the British courts, a case can still be taken to the European Court if the person does not agree with the British court's ruling.

For many years, some politicians and individuals have believed that the European Court of Human Rights should not be able to force changes on British law. They believe that Britain's record on respecting human rights is far better than many other countries.

● The Houses of Parliament in London

Other groups think it is very important that the European Convention became part of British law. This is because there have been many cases where the European Court has found that the British government has violated human rights.

Europe increasingly laying down the law

B

A

Activities

1 **a** In small groups, write your own list of ten human rights.

   b Share your ideas with the rest of the class and agree on a master class set of ten human rights.

2 On your own, look at pictures A and B above. Decide which human right each picture shows. Present your ideas to the rest of the class.

3 Read the information on page 43 and the newspaper headline above. Discuss the following points:

   a What difference did the 1998 Human Rights Act make to people in the UK?

   b Do you think the European Court of Human Rights should be able to influence British laws?

   c Do you agree with the headline?

   d Why do you think the newspaper editor wrote that headline?

4 Write your own newspaper headline and short article explaining the possible effects of the 1998 Human Rights Act in the UK in the future.

Extension activities

5 **a** Go to www.heinemann.co.uk/hotlinks and log on to the United Nations website. Find the simple English version of the Universal Declaration of Human Rights.

   b Copy and complete a large table like the one below. Use it to summarize each article of the declaration. The first two articles have been completed for you.

Article	Human right
1	Requirement to respect rights.
2	Right to life.

6 Compare your master list of ten human rights with the ones summarized in your table. Are there any similarities or differences? Copy and complete a large table like the one below to explain your ideas.

Similarities	Differences

What do I know about human rights in the UK?

Do refugees get a fair deal in the UK?

In the UK, the right for someone to seek asylum is guaranteed under the Universal Declaration of Human Rights. This means that if a person is being badly treated in their own country, they can come to live in the UK.

However, during recent years some politicians and individuals have suggested that the large numbers of people coming to the UK are not all genuine asylum seekers. They say many of them are economic migrants. This means that they are coming to the UK to take advantage of better jobs, higher pay and better healthcare. Some people are worried that they are taking these benefits away from the British people.

The Refugee Council works with asylum seekers and refugees in the UK. The council tries to make sure that refugees and asylum seekers receive caring and fair treatment. Go to www.heinemann.co.uk/hotlinks to look at the Refugee Council's website

● This is a refugee family from Albania

Why do people become refugees?

Leaving your home, family and all your belongings to become a refugee in a strange country is not an easy step. Your future may not be certain because you can be sent home if your appeal fails. Your rights are not the same as the rest of the population in the country.

For example, refugees do not have the right to vote. Many people are forced to become refugees because they have spoken out against their own country's government, or because they wish to be free to follow their own religious beliefs.

Case study 2: Farid Ahmad

Farid Ahmad is a 16-year-old boy living in west London. In 2000, his mother urged him to leave Afghanistan to stop him getting caught up in the civil war there. He trekked – by foot and by lorry – finally reaching England in January 2001.

'On my way to the UK I faced hundreds of problems. I walked for several hours in deserts, mountains, in dark nights, in forests, rain, cold weather and hunger. I spent many nights underground without any bed or blanket with very little food to survive on. I feared and worried for my life. But I was not upset for myself because I am a man and a man never gives up. I think I was on my way for more than two months.'

● Adapted from the BBC News website, 18 October 2001

At the end of 2001 and early 2002 he watched the television coverage of the bombing of Afghanistan in horror, not knowing where his mother and sisters are.

'I do not know the whereabouts of my family and I miss them very much. I feel safe but I am not happy. I hate terrorism, killing of innocent people and shooting of human beings.'

How can Britain cope with the increasing numbers of refugees?

The treatment of refugees in the UK is covered by the 1999 Immigration and Asylum Act. Many human rights organizations believe this act has resulted in unfair treatment for genuine asylum seekers.

Improve conditions in their country

Accept them all

Send them all home

● Some of the ways that Britain could deal with refugees

Activities

In pairs, discuss the following questions.

1. Read the information about the role of the Refugee Council on page 45. Read the three statements above giving some views about how Britain could deal with refugees. Do you agree with any of the views given? You might have a different idea of your own. Explain your answer.

2. There are rights that British citizens have that are not guaranteed for refugees. Discuss which of the following rights you think refugees should have.
   a The right to work.
   b The right to medical care.
   c The right to vote.
   d The right to own a house.
   e The right to education.

3. When they arrive in a country, refugees often come with nothing. Discuss what the UK government should provide for them. Share your ideas with the rest of the class.

Is there equality of opportunity in Britain?

Equality of opportunity means that all people have the same chances in education and in work. For equality of opportunity to exist in Britain, there must be no discrimination against people for any reason. However, it is clear from media reports that discrimination based on race, sex, age and disability does exist in Britain.

Protection against discrimination in Britain is guaranteed under the 1998 Human Rights Act. There are many agencies working in Britain to prevent all forms of discrimination.

One such agency is the Commission for Racial Equality. This was set up under the Race Relations Act 1976 to tackle racial discrimination and promote racial equality. You can get to their website via www.heinemann.co.uk/hotlinks.

COMMISSION FOR RACIAL EQUALITY

Getting technical

Discrimination unfair treatment based on prejudice.

Racial discrimination discrimination based on a person's race or colour.

Sexual discrimination discrimination based on a person's sex.

Age discrimination discrimination based on a person's age.

Media this includes TV, radio, newspapers, magazines and the Internet.

Now you're over the hill

Patrick Grattan of the Third Age Employment Network, says: 'Evidence shows that there is a dramatic drop in the number of people employed once they become older. It's not only a question of people not getting jobs. Even when they do, they're being paid less.'

City analyst claims bias over junior's £1m bonus

A senior City analyst is seeking compensation from her former employers after discovering that her male junior earned a £1 million bonus – more than three times the size of her own.

Van driver unfairly disciplined

A black van driver unfairly disciplined at work has become one of the first people to benefit from the formation of a new racial discrimination legal advice unit. Kofi Asiedu was physically assaulted by his line manager in August last year, following an argument over a delivery.

Do the victims of crime have enough rights?

● People who have been accused of a crime are protected under certain human rights

It does not matter how serious the crime is that has been committed. Human rights legislation gives protection to criminals, both before and after their trial. The 1998 Human Rights Act guarantees the accused the following rights:

- Article 5 – the right to liberty
- Article 6 – the right to a fair trial.

If found guilty of a crime, their rights are still protected and they are guaranteed the following rights:

- Article 3 – the prevention of torture or inhumane punishment
- Article 7 – the right to no punishment without the law.

Who looks after the rights of the victims?

The rights of criminals are protected by the 1998 Human Rights Act, but who looks after the victims' rights?

Case study 3: The murder of Constance Davies

LIFE FOR BURGLAR WHO MURDERED OAP

A man has been jailed for life for the murder of an 87-year-old spinster who died after he attacked her during a break-in at her home.

Simon Taylor of Cardiff denied murder but admitted pushing retired police secretary Constance Davies during a robbery in which he stole £350 from her handbag.

Miss Davies, who was just 4ft 11ins tall, was left for dead after being struck on the head in the attack at her home in Cardiff on 27 August, 2001. In what was described as a 'sudden and brutal' attack, Taylor battered Miss Davies about the head and she fell to the floor, breaking her hip.

The pensioner's health and state of mind went downhill during the next 12 weeks in hospital. She died on 27 October 2001 from a chest infection which, the court heard, was linked to the attack.

● Adapted from the BBC News website, 12 September 2002

Activities

1. Imagine yourself as a child refugee in the UK who has fled from the war in Afghanistan.
   a. In small groups, discuss how you might feel being in a strange country on your own.
   b. On your own, write a letter to your parents in Afghanistan telling them how you feel.

2. Write a list of questions you think a journalist could ask a refugee family to show the difficulties the family faces.

3. Read the newspaper articles on page 47. In small groups, discuss each one and decide the answers to the following questions.
   a. How is the person being discriminated against?
   b. What type of discrimination is taking place?

4. Read the case study about Constance Davies. Which of Miss Davies human rights were taken away from her? Do you believe victims receive enough support? Explain your answer.

What are my rights and responsibilities?

When did education become a right for all children?

Today in the UK all children have the right to an education until the age of 16. It is their parents' responsibility to make sure they attend school. Going to school became law for all children in the 1870s. Before then, many children worked in factories and down mines.

When schools were first set up, some of the methods used by teachers are today considered to conflict with the rights of the child.

Dunce's cap

In the early part of the twentieth century, if their work was not good enough, school children could be made to stand on a stool at the back of the class, wearing an armband with 'Dunce' written on it. The teacher then took a tall, cone-shaped hat with a large 'D' on it, and placed this on the child's head.

The cane

Teachers also punished children by hitting them with a stick called a cane. This was done for many reasons, including rude conduct, leaving the playground without permission, sulkiness, fighting, answering back, and being late. Boys were caned across their bottoms, and girls across their hands or bare legs. Some teachers hit so hard they broke the cane and some kept canes in jars of water to make them more supple, which would sting the child more. Pupils sometimes had to choose which cane they wished to be beaten with! Use of the cane was finally banned in state schools in 1987.

Activities

1. School days are often referred to as 'the happiest days of your life'. Read the information about the dunce's cap and the cane. Discuss how these punishments might have affected you if they were still in use in your school.

2. Imagine yourself standing in the corner of the room wearing a dunce's cap. Write about how you feel. What would you think of your school and your teacher?

3. Look at the list of things that could have meant being caned. What punishment would you get today for similar behaviour?

4. Some adults believe caning should be brought back. Do you agree or disagree with this? Give reasons for your answer.

5. In small groups, role-play a short lesson in Victorian times. One pupil should act as the teacher and the rest should act as pupils. After the role-play, discuss the following points with other groups.
   a What were the pupils' rights?
   b What were the teacher's rights?
   c Did the rights of the teacher ever clash with the rights of the pupils? If so, whose rights are the most important?

How should schools deal with bullies?

Today in school one of the most common problems to be solved is bullying. Being bullied is an attack on human rights. For example, picking on someone because of the colour of their skin is discrimination. Bullying can affect people for the rest of their lives. Read the comments below. They were made by two adults who were bullied at school.

I used to try and toughen myself up but it didn't stop the fact that I used to get jumped on regularly.

I don't think bullies remember who they bullied. It is the bullied who remember who the bullies were.

● Bullying is a common problem in school

Bullying can take many forms: physical, emotional and verbal. It may consist of one child bullying another. It may involve a group of children against a single child, or groups against other groups. It involves:

- power – the victim feels powerless, the bully feels powerful
- emotion – the victim will be upset, the bully is cool and in control
- compassion – the bully will not care about the feelings and concerns of the victim.

What are my responsibilities?

In school there are many different kinds of responsibilities. Along with the rules that all schools have, there are responsibilities that make the rules work. For example, you should not run around your school. If you are late for your lesson, the responsible thing to do is to walk quickly and safely all the way. There are also the responsibilities that go along with the rights you want to have in school. For example, because pupils have the right to learn, the responsible thing to do is not to disrupt lessons. There are other responsibilities that are not always covered by the rules. These are called 'moral responsibilities'. They are about the fact that you should do the right thing and be fair to other people.

Activities

1. Look at the picture of the pupil being bullied and read the information on page 50. Imagine you are the pupil being bullied. How would you feel? Which of your human rights would be affected? What could you do if this was happening every day? What is your moral responsibility if you see this type of situation happening in your school?

2. Read the description of bullying behaviour. Write an explanation of your own. This should include:
   • a definition of what bullying is
   • information about what you should do if you are bullied
   • what your responsibility is if you see someone else being bullied.
   You might like to include information about how bullying affects someone's human rights.

3. What would your moral responsibility be in each of the following situations?
   a You see a pupil in the playground being bullied, out of sight of the teacher on duty.
   b You find a wallet, containing money and house keys, on the floor in the corridor.
   c Your friend tells you that they have taken the pencil case belonging to another pupil in the class.
   d You have not finished your homework when it is time to hand it in.

Extension activities

4. Log on to the Kidscape or Childline website by going to www.heinemann.co.uk/hotlinks. Use these sites to find out more information about bullying.

5. For the following two activities, write your responsibilities as positive statements. For example, instead of 'do not drop litter' use 'put your litter in the bin'.
   a Write a list of your school rules and the responsibilities that go with each rule.
   b Look back to the master list of human rights you drew up on page 44. For each of the rights, think of the responsibility that goes with it. Produce this as a poster to be displayed in the classroom.

How are children's rights protected?

In 1989 the human rights that apply to children were set out in one document. This explained the rights to which every child is entitled, regardless of where they were born, their sex, religion, or social origin. These rights were called the Convention on the Rights of the Child.

A child's right to work

Here is an extract from the convention. It is about the conditions of work for children:

> *The child has the right to be protected from being used to make a profit and from performing work that might be hazardous or interfere with the child's education.*

What rights do children have in the twenty-first century?

A

B

C

D

Activities

1 Look at pictures A–D. For each one, discuss the rights of the children shown.

2 As shown in picture B, many children around the world still work as child labourers instead of going to school. Imagine yourself like this. Write a letter to a friend in the UK, describing your thoughts and feelings while you are working.

3 Read the jobs done by the four children below. For each one, decide if their job should be legal or not.
  a John is 11. His school day finishes at 3.30 pm. He starts his newspaper round straight after school.
  b Sanjeet, who is 16, works two hours on Tuesday evenings and four hours on Saturdays in a local supermarket.
  c Paula is 15. She works behind the bar in a local pub every evening except Sunday.
  d Jennifer, aged 13, delivers newspapers between 4 pm and 5 pm Monday to Friday.

4 Make your own list of twenty rights every child should have. Discuss your rights as a class and agree on a class list of twenty rights.

5 Picture D shows two children in their family home. Write two lists: one showing what you think your parents' responsibilities are, and the other explaining your responsibilities in the home.

Extension activity

6 Use the Internet to find out about children's working conditions around the world. Use the Unicef and Save the Children websites by going to www.heinemann.co.uk/hotlinks.

What happens when human rights are denied?

Although the Universal Declaration of Human Rights was introduced in 1948, there have been many countries which have ignored them. Many countries use torture as part of their treatment of prisoners.

Genocide in Rwanda

There has been trouble in Rwanda between the main ethnic groups – the Tutsis and the Hutus – for many years. In 1994 the plane carrying the Hutu President Juvenal Habyarimana was shot down. The Hutus blamed the Tutsis. Rwanda became the centre for one of the worst acts of genocide since the Second World War. Hutus massacred 800,000 Tutsi men, women and children.

Getting technical

Genocide killing all the people of one ethnic group.

Some countries do not allow people to do the jobs they want to do, or to follow the religion they choose. Some countries have allowed certain groups of people to be murdered.

● Rwanda is a small country in Africa

Case study 4: Hamis Kamuhanda

Hamis Kamuhanda was just 11 years old when the Hutu President was killed. He described how the Hutus entered his home one night. They dragged his father out by his legs. That was the last time he saw him alive. The Hutus then started firing guns into the house. Hamis described the scene:

The bullets came in and hit everything in the way. Yet no one dared scream. I could feel blood coming from under my right shoulder and I did not know whether I was hit or not. I could not feel any pain then. My mind was occupied with the terror of being hacked to death.

Hamis and his family played 'dead', praying the killers would disappear.

Suddenly the door burst open and the gunmen entered the room. Hamis went on to explain what happened next:

I was closer to the door and they kicked me in my belly. It was painful but the thought of being severed alive with their machetes made me stay as quiet as a mouse. One of them said: 'Let's make sure that he is dead with this.' I didn't move an inch, nor did I make any noise. I just felt a very sharp pain in my leg and I must have passed out. When I woke up, my mother was nursing my wounded leg.

Hamis survived his ordeal, even though he lost his right leg.

But he still has hopes for the future. He shares a dream with a friend, who also lost a leg in the genocide, of setting up an athletics team that can represent Rwanda at the Paralympics.

● Adapted from the BBC News website, 2 April 2001

1 Discuss what you think Hamis's thoughts and feelings might have been:

  a as the bullets came towards him
  b about the Hutus who killed his father
  c about the rest of the Hutus living in Rwanda.

Ethnic cleansing in Bosnia

Between 1992 and 1995, human rights in Bosnia were abused in a terrible way. The Serbian people in Bosnia wanted to get rid of other ethnic groups. These people were driven from their homes. Many thousands of Bosnian men were rounded up and held prisoner in camps like Omarska. There, they were starved, beaten and tortured. In the town of Srebrenica in 1995, all the men and boys were rounded up. There were seven thousand in total and they were marched out of the town and shot.

● Bosnian men suffering during the Bosnian war

● Bosnia is a country in the former Yugoslavia

Getting technical

Ethnic cleansing the removal from a country of a group of people of one ethnic origin by another group of people of different ethnic origin. Ethnic cleansing also means killing a group of people of one ethnic origin.

The two main Serbs held responsible for many of the human rights abuses were Radovan Karadzic (who led the government) and Ratko Mladic (who was the general in charge of the army). Today these men are still in hiding, but they are charged by the UN with crimes against humanity. So far, the only Serbian leader to stand trial is Slobodan Milosevic. He is charged with genocide in the Bosnian war.

Case study 5: Zlata Filipovic

From September 1991 to October 1993, Zlata Filipovic, an 11-year-old girl living in Sarajevo, Bosnia, wrote a diary about how the war changed her life and the lives of people around her.

Over the months, Zlata had to cope with the shelling of her home town. Many of her friends and relations left Bosnia to begin their lives elsewhere as refugees. But Zlata and her parents stayed behind. She spent a lot of time with her family in the cellar, sheltering from the bombing. When a friend was killed, Zlata wrote:

Nina, an innocent 11-year-old – the victim of a stupid war. I feel sad. I cry and wonder why? She didn't do anything. A disgusting war destroyed a young girl's life.

Food was scarce and, as winter approached, heating and cooking became difficult. There was no electricity and no water. Zlata wrote how her father got frostbite when he was cutting wood to keep them all warm:

Daddy's got frostbite on his fingers from cutting the wood in the cold cellar. They look awful. His fingers are swollen and now they're putting some cream on them, but they itch badly. Poor Daddy.

● *Zlata's Diary: A Child's Life in Sarajevo* was published in 1994.

Activities

1 Read carefully the information about the genocide in Rwanda and the case study of Hamis Kamuhanda on page 53. How do you feel when you read his story? Explain your answer.

2 Read the case study about Zlata Filipovic. Write an entry for her diary explaining how she felt during the winter in the cold cellar. What did she do? How did she try to keep warm?
   a In pairs, discuss the ten most important things you would expect to find in your home.
   b Now imagine someone wants to move you out and destroy your home. How would you feel? Share your ideas with the rest of the class.

Extension activity

3 a Use the Internet to find out more about the role played by Slobodan Milosevic, Radovan Karadzic and Ratko Mladic in the human rights abuses that took place in Bosnia. Go to www.heinemann.co.uk /hotlinks and click on this activity.
   b List the human rights abuses they are accused of and write a summary of what happened in Bosnia.
   c Report your findings back to the class.

Whose rights are more important?

- Street close circuit TV

- Homes under flight path

- Media coverage of people

Activities

1. Look at pictures A–D. For each picture, explain how the rights of some people are affected by the rights of others.

2. Many pupils like playing football, others do not, explain how your school could solve the conflicting rights of the two groups.

3. Can you think of situations in your school where there are conflicting rights between an individual and a group? How are these solved?

4. Many landowners put up signs saying 'Private property: keep off'. Discuss how this affects the rights of others to enjoy the countryside. How could the rights of both groups be met?

5. Write a newspaper report about a proposal to install security cameras in your local town centre. In your article, explain why the police want the cameras and why some local people are against them.

Which organizations help protect human rights?

There are many international, government and voluntary organizations around the world whose aim is to support human rights.

- UN Refugee Agency

- Oxfam

- United Nations Children's Fund (UNICEF)

Activities

1. a Go to www.heinemann.co.uk/hotlinks and use the Internet to find out about the work of one of the organizations shown above. Report your findings back to the rest of the class.
   b Design a new logo and slogan for your selected organization.

2. Copy and complete a large table like this one for the organizations shown above and find out about some other organizations.

Organization	What does it do?

3. Many of the organizations supporting human rights are charities. In pairs, discuss why it is important for people to support the work of such organizations. Share your ideas with the rest of the class.

Review and reflect

In this chapter you have learned about human rights. You have learned about the rights of children. You have also learned how in some parts of the world human rights are being abused.

Days to reflect on human rights

There are days each year which have been set aside to remember people or events relating to human rights. Each country has its own memorial days that are important to the people living there. Here are a few examples:

- International Human Rights Day
- United Nations Day
- UNICEF Day of Change
- Holocaust Memorial Day
- Martin Luther King Day.

● Martin Luther King, a civil rights campaigner in America in the 1960s

Getting technical

Civil rights the rights of people to political and social freedom.

Activities

1 **a** Use the Internet to find out more about each of the special days listed above.
b Copy and complete a large table like this one listing each of the special days mentioned above.

Special day	Date	Purpose

2 Visit the Holocaust Memorial Day website. Go to www.heinemann.co.uk/hotlinks and read the organization's aims before discussing the following questions.
a Do you agree with these aims?
b How do you think the Holocaust Memorial Day helps achieve these aims?
c What could be done to stop the genocides which still take place across the world?

3 Draw a timeline from 1900 to today on which all the dates for human rights legislation you have read about are shown. For each piece of legislation, include its title and a summary of what it was about.

4 Look at the two contrasting pictures above. Discuss the human rights they represent and then identify the advantages we have in the UK. What other advantages do we have?

Extension activity

5 **a** In pairs, discuss if you would like to see a Children's Rights Day celebrated at your school.
b If so, decide when should it be held and what special things should happen on that day.
c Can you think of any stories about particular people around the world which could help celebrate the rights of children?
d Are there any rights you think should be highlighted?

Chapter 4

Crime and punishment

Learn about...

In recent years, a number of media reports have highlighted increases in crime statistics. In this chapter we will look at some of the factors which contribute to criminal activity and how the criminal justice system deals with juveniles.

- What is the role of the modern police force?
- What is a crime, who is a criminal and what are the effects of crime?
- How does criminal behaviour change with age and sex?
- What are the causes of crime and the age of criminal responsibility?
- What are your rights if you are arrested?
- What is the difference between adult and juvenile courts?
- What is involved in the sentencing of juveniles and what is life like inside a young offenders' centre?
- How are juveniles stereotyped by the media and other adults?

Getting technical

Media this includes TV, radio, newspapers, magazines and the Internet.

Crime any action which is against the law.

Criminal someone who has committed a crime.

Criminal justice system the system where suspected criminals are tried in a court.

Juvenile someone under the age of 17.

Police the force responsible for keeping law and order.

Stereotype an unjustified and fixed standard image of a person.

Activities

1 Look at these two media reports. Discuss the image each report gives of the police and young people.

Half of all young people have 'committed crime'

Man claims he confessed after police torture

2 Look at the first report.

- **a** How many pupils in your class does the report suggest have committed a crime?
- **b** Do you think half the pupils in your class have committed a crime?
- **c** How many pupils in your class know someone who has committed a crime?
- **d** Does the report give a fair image of the young?

3
- **a** What do you think is the role of the police?
- **b** How well do these reports suggest the police are doing in carrying out their role?
- **c** Do these reports give a fair image of the police?

What is the job of the police force?

Activities

1. Some people feel it is better for the police to concentrate on preventing crime. In pairs, discuss these questions.
   a How can the police prevent crime?
   b Do you agree that crime prevention is more important than crime detection?

2. Write a list of instructions for younger pupils explaining how, if they needed to, they could contact the police. Design a poster to stress the importance of only calling the emergency services when it is a true emergency.

3. a Go to www.heinemann.co.uk/hotlinks and log on to the New Westminster Police Service website. Read the nine principles that Robert Peel, the founder of the modern police force, believed were needed for the police to function properly.
   b In small groups, discuss these principles and decide how important you think they are to the modern police force.

4. Use the Internet to find out about your local police force. Who is the Chief Constable? Where are their headquarters? What are their aims?

What is a criminal offence?

Everyone will – at some time or another – have committed a criminal offence, although in most cases only in a minor way. For example, have your parents ever broken the speed limit? Crimes of this nature and other minor types are being committed all the time. Even being present when a crime is taking place can mean you are guilty of the same crime.

Are minor crimes acceptable? What difference does it make if the speed limit is broken by just 5mph? Can you think of any other minor crimes?

As long as there is not an accident, this type of crime is victimless – no one has lost anything or suffered because of it.

But other crimes are more serious. These are usually crimes where there is a victim who suffers because of the criminal's actions. For example, if your parents hit someone with the car while speeding, this would be viewed as a serious crime.

Getting technical

Offence an illegal action.
Victim the person who has been affected by a crime.

Who is a criminal?

Some actions have an age restriction below which it is illegal to do them. For example, it is against the law to drive a car on the road before the age of 17.

How old do you have to be to buy fireworks?

How old do you have to be to buy cigarettes?

How old do you have to be to buy alcohol in a shop?

How old do you have to be to buy a lottery ticket?

How old do you have to be to buy alcohol in a pub?

How old do you have to be to drive a car?

Activities

1 Look carefully at the picture opposite. Discuss the following questions.

  a Are all the actions shown crimes?

  b Which crimes are serious and which are minor?

  c Does each crime have a victim? If so, who is the victim?

  d How might the crime affect any victims?

  e Which crimes have no victims? Where there are no victims, discuss how the offence might affect the person committing the crime.

2 **a** Discuss the questions around the picture above and decide on the answers. Check the correct answers with your teacher.

  b Discuss how serious each action is and what the consequences might be of breaking the law in each case. For each question, decide if there is someone else responsible for the crime. If so, who is responsible and what should happen to them?

3 **a** Go to www.heinemann.co.uk/hotlinks and log on to the BBC News website. Find information about the suggestion to decriminalize cannabis.

  b In pairs, discuss the suggestion that cannabis should be decriminalized. The answers to the following questions might help your discussions.

    • Is cannabis addictive?

    • Is the use of cannabis linked to other crimes?

    • Is cannabis harmful to the person using it?

  c Discuss whether you think each of the following should be against the law:

    • smacking children

    • buying alcohol at the age of 16

    • driving at 80 mph on a motorway.

Getting technical

Decriminalize to no longer be treated as a criminal offence.

What causes people to commit crimes?

Very few people become involved in serious criminal activities the first time they commit a crime. It is usually a gradual process that starts with minor crimes. These can then lead them on to more serious action. This could be because they are looking for excitement or even out of boredom. Sometimes people feel they need to commit crimes because their friends do.

Activities

1. Look at the picture at the top of this page.
   a What crimes are being committed?
   b Who is committing the crime?
   c If you do not want to have a criminal record, what should you do if your friend put you in situations like these?

2. In small groups, discuss the following questions. What is your legal position if a friend tells you about a crime they are going to commit? What should you do? You might like to consider these statements to help you answer the questions.
   a You can be held responsible for the crime.
   b You should do nothing to help commit the crime.
   c You should try to get your friend not to commit the crime.
   d You should tell an adult or the police about your friend's plans.

What factors cause young people to get involved in crime?

How did you get involved in crime?

> I went to the shops with my best friend, Laura. She suggested I get us a chocolate bar while she bought a magazine. It gave us such a buzz, it just went from there and now we go to town on a Saturday and pick up anything we can.

Amy, 13

> I was bored hanging around outside the shops at night with my friends. One day, Jamie suggested smoking some dope, from there I went on to coke. Now I need to steal from cars or houses to pay for my habit.

Jonathan, 17

Activities

1. Read the statements made by Amy and Jonathan above. What factors caused each of them to get involved in crime? What crimes are they involved in?

2. Amy and Jonathan have suggested some reasons why they became involved in crime. Are these reasons, or are they excuses? What is the difference? Whose fault is it that they turned to crime?

3. Write an ending for either Amy's or Jonathan's story.

Extension activity

4. Write a list of any other things you can think of that may lead to criminal activity.

Who commits crime?

Do boys or girls commit more crime?

Graph A shows the numbers of boys and girls, per 100,000 of the population, who were caught involved in criminal activities in 2000 and the age they were at the time.

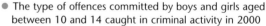

A

- The age of boys and girls caught in criminal activity per 100,000 people in 2000

Does the type of crime differ for boys and girls?

The graphs in B show the types of crime boys and girls aged between 10 and 14, who were caught, were involved in.

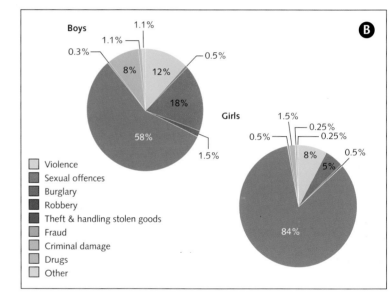

- The type of offences committed by boys and girls aged between 10 and 14 caught in criminal activity in 2000

Activities

1. Look at graph A. In small groups, discuss these questions.
   a. What is the difference between the numbers of boys and girls committing crime?
   b. Why do you think these trends happen?

2. Look at the graphs in B. In small groups, discuss these questions.
   a. Which crimes are committed most often by boys and by girls?
   b. Which crimes do boys and girls commit least often?
   c. Why do you think these trends happen?

3. Following your discussion, report back to the class.

When is a child responsible for their actions?

The need for an age of criminal responsibility is laid down in the United Nations Convention on the Rights of the Child, which states that:

Every child, whether they are innocent or guilty of breaking the law, has the right to treatment to help them understand what has happened and to learn from their mistakes.

However, the age at which a child becomes responsible varies greatly. In some countries it is as low as 7 years old.

The argument over the minimum age of criminal responsibility comes down to whether or not a child

Getting technical

Criminal responsibility when someone is judged to be responsible for their own actions.

should be treated as an adult if they break the law. Children under the age of responsibility are considered to be influenced by many factors that do not apply to adults, for example, peer influence, risk-taking, emotional immaturity. These factors, among other things, mean children do not realistically assess the consequences of their actions and so cannot be held responsible for their actions.

When is a child responsible for their actions in the UK?

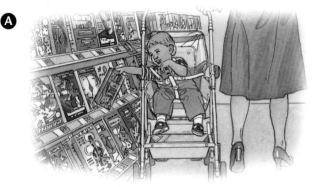

A   **B**

- At what age is a child considered responsible for its actions?
- At what age does a child become an adult in the eyes of the law?

Country	Age of criminal responsibility
Belgium	18
Spain	16
Germany	14
Italy	14
France	13
Canada	12
Netherlands	12
Australia	10
UK	10
USA	7* * In most states

Case study 1: James Bulger

James Bulger, aged 2, was taken away from his mother by two boys while at a butcher's shop in the Bootle Strand Shopping Centre in Liverpool. The two boys took James to a railway line, where they beat and stoned him to death. They left him on the railway track to be cut in half by a train. The two boys, who were aged 10, were later arrested and tried in an adult court.

Case study 2: Damilola Taylor

Damilola Taylor grew up in Nigeria. In August 2000, the 10-year-old boy came to London to live with a relative.

After school on 27 November 2000, Damilola went to a computer club at his local library. As he walked home, he was stabbed and bled to death in a stairwell of a block of flats just a few hundred metres from his home.

Damilola had written an essay, in which he said: 'I want to be the very best, like no one ever has been.'

In June 2001 four youths – one aged 14, two aged 15 and one 16 – were charged with his murder. All four were cleared of murder in 2002.

Activities

1 Look at pictures A and B. In small groups, discuss these questions.
   a What crimes are both children committing?
   b Are they both responsible for their actions?

Discuss at what age you think a child should be responsible for its actions and when you think a child should become an adult in the eyes of the law.

2 Reread the case studies about James Bulger and Damilola Taylor. In small groups, discuss:

Case study 1
- How old were the people accused in the James Bulger case?
- Are children of this age legally responsible for their actions?
- Do children this age know what is wrong?
- Were the two boys old enough to be tried in an adult court?
- What role do you think the media played in the way these two boys were dealt with?

Case study 2
- How old were the people accused in the Damilola Taylor case?
- Are children this old legally responsible for their actions?
- Do children this age know what is wrong?

Extension activities

3 Find out what happened when the accused children in the two case studies were taken to court.

4 **a** Go to www.heinemann.co.uk/hotlinks and use the BBC News website to find other examples of cases when juveniles have been tried in court for serious crimes.
   b Write a newspaper article on the information you have found.

How to...
Write a newspaper article
- Think of a headline that sums up your story.
- The first paragraph should make the reader want to read more.
- The story – remember to explain who is involved, what happened, when and where the events took place and why these things happened.
- In the last paragraph, add any interesting quotes. Remember that if you want to take sides in your article, you can simply use the quotes from the people you agree with and ignore the others.
- Make sure you come to a definite ending.
- Add pictures, tables or charts to your report.

5 Look at the table giving the ages of criminal responsibility around the world.
   a Draw a bar chart to show the information.
   b Which countries have the youngest and oldest ages of responsibility?
   d Which country has the same age of responsibility as Britain?

What are your rights if you are arrested?

When the police arrest a person on suspicion of carrying out a crime, there are certain rights that they must allow that person. The pictures below show some of the stages involved in an arrest. Think of the rights that the person should be allowed at each stage.

Getting technical

Arrest when a person is detained by the legal authorities.

Rights freedoms which everyone has but which can be taken away if convicted of a crime.

Activities

1 Look at pictures A–D. In small groups, discuss the following questions.
  a What do you think is the first thing the police have to do?
  b What do you think the police must allow someone to do when they get to the police station?
  c Who should be present when a juvenile is interviewed by the police? What questions do you think the person who has been arrested must answer?
  d How long do you think the police should be able to keep someone under arrest at the police station before charging or releasing them?

2 Many juveniles are given a reprimand for their first minor offence.
  a What does 'reprimand' mean?
  b What sorts of offences may receive a reprimand?
  c Do you think being given a reprimand means you have a police record?

How are children aged between 10 and 17 dealt with by the juvenile court system?

Children are tried in the youth court, which is part of the magistrate's court. There are special systems in the youth court, which are there to protect the child on trial. There is no public gallery and no journalists are allowed in the courtroom. The child on trial must have a parent or guardian with them.

● An adult court

Getting technical

Magistrate a civil officer who hands out justice.
Solicitor a member of the legal profession qualified to advise a client or a barrister.
Defendant a person accused in a court of law.
Accused a person accused of committing a crime.
Plea a formal statement made by or for a defendant.
Mitigation circumstances used to excuse an action.
Perjury telling a lie when under oath.
Oath a solemn declaration made in court.

● A juvenile court

Activities

1. Draw two spider diagrams like the ones below to show the things you notice about adult and juvenile courts.

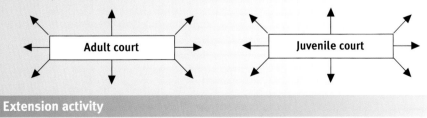

Extension activity

2. Explain why some of these differences exist and how they help to make the trial of a juvenile fair and less frightening.

What sentences are available to the juvenile courts?

People who are convicted of committing crimes can receive a range of different sentences. The sentence given by the court depends on the how serious the crime is.

Sentences for youths are more varied than those for adults, and parents of young people can also be given court orders to stop their children re-offending. There are four main levels of sentence available to the courts, depending on the seriousness of the crime. These are discharges, fines, community sentences and imprisonment. Fines are the most commonly used sentence. Imprisonment is the most severe penalty available to the courts and is only applied to the more serious offences.

Getting technical

Sentence punishment given to a person convicted of committing a crime.

Deterrent fear of punishment that it is hoped will stop people committing crimes again or in the first place.

Retribution the idea that if someone has done something wrong, they should be given a punishment to fit the crime.

Do the courts let young people off lightly?

Case study 3

'Terror triplets' are released

Thirteen-year-old triplets, Shane, Natalie and Sarah Morris, who terrorised shopkeepers in Gillingham, Kent, walked free from court after magistrates gave them a two-year supervision order.

The triplets had been found guilty of breaking an anti-social behaviour order handed down on them a year ago.

The court heard that the three teenagers had kicked the door of a shop and then threatened to put a petrol bomb through the door of a security guard's home.

Shopkeepers in Gillingham had asked magistrates to lock up the youngsters, but lawyers said they were too young to be jailed.

Reacting to the verdict, one shopkeeper said: 'I'm disgusted they will be allowed to go back on the streets and carry on where they left off. This is just a sign to all the other kids that they can do what they like and get away with it.'

Case study 4

Home secretary targets young criminals

Young offenders who keep on committing crimes face being locked up while they are waiting to be tried under new powers given to courts, the Home Secretary has announced.

The move is part of a campaign against street crime and the young criminals who, the Home Secretary says, boast to their friends that they can do anything and still be free the next day.

The Metropolitan Police Commissioner said 'the police are now arresting children as young as 8 for serious offences like robbery.'

At present, teenagers can only be locked up on remand if they are suspected of committing serious or violent offences. Now the powers will be extended to include those accused of crimes like car theft and criminal damage.

The Home Secretary also announced a scheme that orders the parents of unruly teenagers to attend special classes on how to be a good parent.

Activities

1   In small groups, discuss the following questions.
   a   What are the main reasons for sending someone to prison? Explain your answer.
   b   When deciding on the punishment, how far do you think the sentence should act as a deterrent?
   c   When deciding on the punishment, what part do you think retribution should play?
   d   What other reasons can you give for punishment?

2   Copy the following sentences available to a juvenile court, and match up each with the correct meaning.

Sentences
• Anti-social behaviour order
• Police warning
• Reparation order
• Secure remand
• Detention and training order

Meanings
• The juvenile is asked to make amends towards the wrong they have done.
• The juvenile is held in a local authority secure accommodation centre.
• The juvenile is warned by a police officer.
• The juvenile is held in a young offenders' centre.
• To place certain restrictions on the youth not to be involved in certain types of behaviour.

3   Read the definition of mitigation (page 67).
   a   Do you think the following statement could be used as mitigation in a case of assault? 'He looked like he was going to hit me. So I hit him first.'
   b   If not, what do you think could be used as mitigation?

4   Read the case studies on page 68 and 69.
   a   How do you think the triplets should have been punished?
   b   Do you think the Home Secretary's plans are a harsher treatment of young offenders?

Extension activity

5   a   Go to www.heinemann.co.uk/hotlinks and use the BBC News website to find the meaning of the term 'boot camp'.
   b   Discuss the advantages and disadvantages of these types of institutions for punishing juveniles.
   c   Does this type of punishment represent harsh treatment?

Life inside a young offenders centre

Thinking

The clanking of keys, the stamping of feet
Why aren't there people in here I can greet?
I'm lonely and cold with no one to love
Eyes look coldly down from above
My clothes are all ripped, my hair is all matted
I can't seem to sleep, my thoughts are all scattered
Nowhere to walk, nothing to do
Why can't I go and have fun just like you?
The dampness inside, the smell in the air
No one to love, oh it's just not fair
The birds are outside, all singing their song
But I'm stuck in here and the days seem so long.

Greer Holmes, aged 14
Kelvin Hall School, Hull

Real life inside a young offender's centre

I am now nearing the end of my first sentence and let me tell you it will be the last! You often hear other prisoners saying that they will be back. Why? Prison is a mug's game. What joy is there getting everything you possess taken away from you, liberty, family, friends and especially freedom. In civilian life everything is taken for granted, but when you're locked up in a concrete box it suddenly hits you: you have nothing, you are as low as you can possibly get.

Getting technical

Censors people whose job it is to read personal letters, taking out any parts they think should not be sent.

The following information is part of an inmate's Saturday morning routine.

0730	Roll check
0800–0825	Breakfast (including medical treatments)
0845–0945	Exercise in yard (for vulnerable prisoners)
0855	Inmates leave for visits (if one has been booked)
0900	Outgoing mail to censors
0900–1000	Cell cleaning or stay in cell
1000–1100	Main exercise or stay in cell
1100	Lock up
1145–1230	Dinner (including medical treatments)
1230	Roll check and lock up

What is the role of a young offenders' centre?

Deterrent? Reform? Protection? Punishment?

Young offenders' centres place a great deal of emphasis on education and training in the hope of giving the offenders the skills and qualifications to avoid re-offending once they have finished their sentence and are released.

Activities

1. Read the poem called 'Thinking' and the real-life story. In small groups, discuss how you think you might feel inside the young offenders' centre.

2. Write a letter to your family telling them of your life in the centre and how you feel.

3. Look at the picture showing electronic tagging.
   a What is electronic tagging?
   b What effect does it have?

4. The role of the young offenders' centre could be described as deterrent, reform, protection or punishment.
   a Discuss with a partner the meaning of each role.
   b Put them in order of importance for:
   • the public
   • the prison service
   • the inmate.

   Share your ideas with the rest of the class.

How do adults view juveniles?

● William Cavener

● John Smith

'Vigilante' concern on estate

Residents on a north Wales housing estate have voiced their concerns at possible vigilante action to stop a gang of youths. People living on the estate say some residents have begun patrolling the area to stop vandalism and violence.

Councillor Derek Hainge said buses had been attacked by youths and forced off the road and pensioners homes had been attacked. 'People have just got so frustrated at the lack of action,' he said. 'This is a very real concern. It only takes a split second for someone to pull a knife and hurt someone. We do not want people here to get hurt.'

Sylvia Humphreys, a city councillor, said she had also grown concerned by events. 'There are residents who are 70, 80 and 90 years old who do not want this; they are frightened to open their doors. These men who have been going out on patrol have been doing more than the police and if they are not doing any harm, good luck to them.'

Activities

1. Look at the pictures of John Smith and William Cavener. In small groups, discuss these questions.

   a What do you think their home life is like?
   b What type of school do you think the boys attend?
   c What sort of qualifications do you think they will get?
   d Which of these two pupils might have a criminal record?
   e What crime do you think he could have commited?
   f Why do you think he might have committed this crime?

Police still search more black people

Black people are now eight times more likely to be stopped and searched by the police than white people according to the latest Home Office figures.

Activities

1. What does the word 'stereotype' mean?

2. a Discuss with the rest of the class your answers to **a–f** and how they could have been influenced by stereotypical images.
   b Read the information in the article above. How would you feel as a young person living on that estate?

3. Read the information on police stop and search figures in the second article. Why do you think the police stop more black people? How you would feel if you were stopped by the police when you had done nothing wrong.

Extension activities

4. Imagine you were stopped by the police when you had done nothing wrong. Write a short poem about how you feel when you are stopped and when the police officer is searching you.

5. The media often gives high priority to reports of unruly teenagers. Read case study 3 on page 68.
   a Which words are used to give a negative image?
   b Go to www.heinemann.co.uk/hotlinks and log on to the BBC News website and search for similar reports. Make a list of any words you find that are used to create a negative image. Then think of a positive word for each negative word.

6. Write a newspaper article about an event that has happened recently in your local area, giving a positive image of teenagers. Your article can be based on real events or your story can be made up.

Review and reflect

● 'Criminals know they won't go to court'

● 'The courts are too lenient'

Activities

① Look at the pictures on this page. From what you have learned, discuss in small groups if you think these statements are true.

② Read these groups of words and terms.
   a Arrest, police station, plea, interview.
   b Magistrate, jury, parent, solicitor.
   c Peer pressure, alcohol, drugs, theft.
   d Mugging, burglary, graffiti, shoplifting.

For each group, work out which word or term is the odd one out. Explain your answers.

Extension activity

③ Think of some groups of words of your own and test your partner to see if they can find the odd ones out.

● 'Prisons are a holiday camp'

Getting technical

Peer pressure pressure to do the same things as your friends.

Chapter 5

Citizenship and history: voting

Learn about...

In this chapter we will look at society in the UK today. Think for a moment of all the rules that people live by, and think about the rights you and other people have. Whose job is it to make these rules and to protect these rights? What would happen if people disagreed with the way our society is organized and run? How would you feel if you had no say in the way our country was run? How could you change this?

- How can people in society make decisions?
- Why were some people in the UK not allowed to vote in the past, but now they can?
- Why do some people choose not to vote?
- Why is it that some people cannot vote?
- What is the importance of taking an active role in a democratic country?

Getting technical

Vote to show your view on something.
Democratic the idea that everyone's opinions are as important as anyone elses.

A story of survival

The survivors
Earth date: 2402

An eerie, unnatural light was cast by the twin moons of Hyperion. The featureless landscape was stark and unwelcoming, the dusty surface rippled only by the odd gust of wind, the silence broken only by our footsteps.

It had taken fifteen years of travel to get here. Our craft had successfully landed on this unwelcoming planet while we, its crew, slowly emerged from stasis, that strange half-life which is the curse of space travel.

Primary probes had told us that this new world could support life. Early tests confirmed this. A spaceship's remains lay before me, crashed on the planet's surface. The crew had left two earth years before us, but no contact was made after their craft, Excalibur, left orbit. We had come to discover what had happened to them. The bare hulk of twisted metal was our only welcome, the ghostly remains of a once fine starship.

What became of its passengers was a mystery. It was our mission to solve this mystery. Further investigation of the wreckage yielded some of its secrets. It became clear that all the adult members of the group were unlikely to have survived the impact. Their stasis pods were located in the stern of the ship and bore the full brunt of the impact. Such damage to a space-sleep pod would remove any protection, and any who emerged would have died.

The children's quarters, on the other hand, were at the rear of the craft. Closer examination of this area made us think that at least a few of these young travellers had survived.

Inside were log entries made by young crew members in the days that followed. They were incomplete, but told us enough to guess at the problems and challenges which faced this group of now orphaned young people. They were alone and friendless on a desolate planet, many light years from home.

Reading these entries gave us hope, but some parts were missing. We had to use our brains to fill in the gaps, to find out what happened when a group of young people found themselves alone. For the first time in their lives, they were having to make decisions without older people being around and without the possibility of immediate rescue.

The documents recovered were written by people giving their own accounts of their experiences at the time. We thought it strange that they had chosen this way to communicate. It seemed likely that some sort of breakup had happened between the group members, and that they had each recorded their own thoughts to be sure their views would be considered properly. We would have welcomed help from earth to piece together the story, but we were light years away from that possibility.

Log Entry 1

I am Anna. When I discovered the elders were gone, I knew that there was going to be panic among the little ones. I am saddened at the loss of our loved ones, but my training tells me that feelings are useless in moments of crisis. It is my job to take action. Our choices are clear enough.

Should we stay at the crash site and use what skills we have to repair the ship? Can we survive long enough for a rescue party from earth to find us? They will have the details of our proposed landing – and they will find us more easily if we stay – but time is against us. We must find ways of living in this new world. We must find the resources we need to build shelters and we must find food. Above all, we need to establish some rules. The little ones are already beginning to look lost. Someone must be given the task of looking after them and keeping them safe.

My first task will be to call a meeting and put myself forward as leader. I come from a family of the highest rank, so it is right that I take command. It is, after all, in my blood.

WARNING: REMAINING PART OF ENTRY 1 HAS BEEN CORRUPTED

Log Entry 2

I am Zeref. I have agreed to make a statement so that the truth can be known. There are only 25 viable survivors. The others are useless, either whining kids or doddering old ones, unfit to waste our dwindling food supplies on.

My team is strong and able. They have identified me as one who can lead a successful expedition to find a suitable location for a new base. Most of the others see the wisdom of this plan. We could quickly establish what resources this planet can offer, and use them to have some sort of life again instead of waiting round like androids who programmers have left on standby! We will leave the old ones behind and set up a new community under my leadership. I am the best leader here as I am the strongest of the survivors. My way is the only way – anyone who does not want my leadership can find their own way of survival.

WARNING: REMAINING PART OF ENTRY 2 HAS BEEN CORRUPTED

Log Entry 3

I am Demetrius. We need to work together as an organized group with a clear focus on what we hope to achieve. We need to find out which areas are suitable for us to establish a settlement, but the little ones and the elders could not cope with a trek through the wilderness with no clear destination.

Each person has something to contribute, and we must decide together what should be done. I do not wish to take sole control. I will propose that an inner council is formed. This council will give roles to each of us, according to our skills.

We must have a plan to care for the old ones. Those poor souls have no memories of the journey and their bodies are frail. Gone for ever are the strong and brave travellers who were our guardians and guides. They deserve our protection now.

The little ones will grow wild if we do not think of some kind of programme for them. Those who are most skilled must pass on their knowledge, so that our group can grow and gradually establish a society here.

WARNING: REMAINING PART OF ENTRY 3 HAS BEEN CORRUPTED

Activities

In small groups, discuss the following questions.

1 The three people in the log entries each have a different view of how society should be organized. Thinking about their personalities, choose three words to describe each of them. You can use some of the words below or any others you can think of.

   resourceful • rude • caring • determined • adventurous • tough • fair • doubting • democratic • sentimental • inventive • brave • trustworthy • ruthless • sharing • brutal

2 How do you think each person will try to lead the community?

3 What qualities do you think a good leader should have?

4 How will the community make decisions under each person's leadership?

5 How do you think Anna, Zeref and Demetrius would deal with people who have different opinions from them?

6 Think back to a situation where you were not allowed to express an opinion about a decision that affected you, either at school or at home. What was this decision? How did you feel about being left out?

7 Reread Zeref's log entry.
   a Which groups of people might feel left out?
   b What sort of emotions will these people be feeling on the planet?

Read the next part of the story.

The survivors (continued)

We tried to work out the missing sections of the log entries, with limited success. We worked out that a leadership struggle occurred within days of the entries being written. Which one of the three was successful we did not yet know.

We began to get readings from an area of the planet which we thought might be fertile. We decided to go there and meet the survivors of the *Excalibur*, assuming they were the life forms our equipment had detected.

My team members and I thought about what might have happened and worked out theories about how each of the young possible leaders may have behaved. We asked ourselves questions about how each of them would have reacted to different situations. One of our concerns was how they would have reacted to opposition. We would soon know.

Three weeks later, we stood on the brow of a hill staring down at a valley full of light.

Activities

1. Who do you think would have emerged as leader?

2. What sort of society do you think they would be leading?

3. Draw a picture or write an story about what you think the rescuers would have found when they walked down from the hill on the planet of Hyperion.

4. Write down three questions for another group to discuss. Swap these, then join up as a large group to compare answers.

Extension activity

5. Work with a group of classmates to set up a drama scene of a few different situations on the planet (for example, discussions about what sort of political system there should be). You may need to take the parts of Anna, Zeref and Demetrius. Other characters can be added if you like. Your role-play could be videoed or tape-recorded for other pupils to watch later.

Your school manifesto

All schools should try to get the opinions of their pupils. One way of doing this is by having a school council. Explain the role of school councils by answering the following questions. You may need to do some research to find the answers.

- Name five members of a school council.
- What does a school council do?
- How does a school council take into account the opinions of all pupils?
- What influence does a school council have?

Getting technical

Manifesto a public declaration of aims.

School councils may help to develop the rights of pupils, but they should also help with understanding other people's rights. Schools are places where many different groups of people go to learn or to work. All these people will have some ideas about the rights they expect from their school.

Activities

1 In groups, do some research about the rights that people would like to have in school. Interview a few different people, such as teachers, pupils, canteen staff, cleaning staff, office staff, local residents and local shopkeepers. You will need to draw up a questionnaire, and you may like to use tape recorders and videos. Remember to ask people's permission if you are going to record or film them.

How to...
Produce a questionnaire
- Make a draft of the questions you would like to ask before you start.
- Think of about 5 to 10 questions at the most.
- Use a mixture of questions that should be answered 'yes' or 'no', and questions that need longer answers.
- Make sure you write the name of the person you are interviewing at the top of each questionnaire so that you can analyse the results later.
- Remember to thank each person for their time when you have finished.

2 Find a way of presenting your findings to a range of people and especially to the people you interviewed. You might like to draw some posters that can be displayed in and around the school, or you could produce a leaflet to be handed out.

3 Write a report for your school community which explains what you have found out about school rights. Give your report the title 'Manifesto of Rights'. Include a summary of the main rights that each of the groups interviewed feel they should be entitled to. This could start 'We believe we should have the right to...'. You could use ICT for your report if you like.

Case study 1: School councils – what can they achieve?

The School Council of Featherstone High School in West London has already achieved a number of successes. It holds fundraising events so that the Year 11 pupils can have a leavers' party every year. The council also organizes this.

The school council is made up of representatives from the various year councils. Each year council has a male and a female representative from each class. In the future, the school council plans to deal with issues such as litter around the school. It plans to give information to teachers about what aspects of school life really help pupils to learn well. The council has a budget, which it must account for. Each year it sends representatives to the regional youth parliament.

Getting technical

Representative someone elected to put across other people's views.
Citizen an active member of a community.

Activities

In small groups, complete the following research project. You will need a copy of your school's prospectus or advertising literature.

Blue Hall High School

Quality Education for all

See inside for information of our improving exam results and new computer suite

1 What claims does your school make to parents about your development while you are at the school?

2 Do you agree that these claims are correct and worthwhile? Explain your views.

3 Do you feel that your school is doing what it says it will do? Explain your answer.

4 Would you like to change your school's prospectus? If so, how?

5 Read the following statements and say how your school is helping you to develop the skills of being a citizen.
   a 'The most basic principle of citizenship is that people should govern themselves.'
   b 'Education should fully develop human personality and strengthen respect for human rights and freedoms. It should promote understanding, tolerance and friendship among countries and racial or religious groups. It should try to bring about peace.'

6 What more do you think your school could do in order to help you develop these skills further?

Can't vote, won't vote

Can't vote

In 1831 the only people who were allowed to vote in the UK were some wealthy men who owned property. Millions of people had no say in how their lives were run. In those days, Members of Parliament (MPs) did not represent the views of the people in their areas.

Gradually, more and more people were given the franchise – the right to vote. Many people fought very hard for this. By 1928 all men and women had equal rights to vote. At last the UK had become a democratic society and MPs had become representatives of all the people in their areas.

Getting technical

Franchise the right to vote in elections.
Apathy lack of interest.

Won't vote

These days, there are many opportunities for every citizen to have a view on how the UK is governed. These views can be put across in different ways, from writing letters and having meetings to voting. Everyone over the age of 18 is allowed to vote (with a few exceptions, such as prisoners and patients in mental health hospitals). However, some people choose not to vote. Although this is their right, many people feel this apathy is wrong.

In the last general election in 2001, only 59 per cent of the people who could have voted did so. Out of the people who were aged between 18 and 24 years old, only 39 per cent of them – just over a third – who could have voted actually did vote.

I didn't know what to do when I got in the polling station.

What's the point – all the parties are the same anyway.

I couldn't get to the polling station in time.

I couldn't be bothered. I might have voted if they had made it easier.

Activities

1 In small groups, carry out your own research on voting. Produce a questionnaire and ask a range of local people about whether they voted or not in the last local, general or European elections. Then ask them for suggestions about what might encourage them to vote in the future.

2 Present your findings and suggestions to a local councillor or your MP. Include some of the suggestions to encourage more people to vote. Make your report as detailed and interesting as possible.

3 **a** What does the word 'apathy' mean?
b What suggestions could you make to convince people to be less apathetic and more involved?

4 List as many reasons as you can think of to explain why some people may decide not to vote.

Review and reflect

● Black South Africans campaigning against apartheid

● People opposing a dictatorship

● Suffragettes used various methods to raise awareness about the unfairness of women not being allowed to vote

Getting technical

Suffragettes a group of women in the early 1900s who used organized protest, and sometimes violence, to campaign for the right to vote.

Activities

1. Think about the activities you have done in this chapter. What have you learned from the activities?

2. Will you use your right to vote when you are 18? Explain your answer.

3. Do you think people who do not use their right to vote should be fined?

4. Do you think you can be a good citizen if you do not use your right to vote? Explain your answer.

5. What do you think will happen in our society if less and less people vote?

6. In which parts of your life would you like to have a greater say?

Extension activities

7. What groups did you work in during this chapter?

8. How well did your group perform?

9. Did your group co-operate with each other and with other groups?

10. **a** What advice could you give other groups so that they can improve next time?
    b What advice have other groups given you?

Chapter 6

Citizenship and history: world peace

Learn about...

In this chapter we will be looking at conflict and peace throughout the world, and how these ideas are shown in newspapers and on television.

- How does the media cover conflict between people and countries?
- Why it is important to have a sense of history in understanding conflict situations?
- How can differences be resolved and what difficulties can arise?
- How do current national and international conflicts affect our world?

Case study 1: Holy Cross Infants School

● Children and their parents on the way to Holy Cross Infants School

Battles and wars are not always between two countries. In September 2001 a battle took place about a road that children walk down with their parents on the way to school.

Over 140 Roman Catholic primary school children and their parents had to pass through Ardoyne, a Protestant area of Belfast, Northern Ireland, to get to school. They had to walk 300 metres along a road which was lined by local people shouting and throwing things at them. Many of the children were upset and frightened. Some of the children were as young as 4 years old.

The Protestants threatened many of the Catholic parents. They said they would kill the Catholics if they took their children down the route.

One BBC news correspondent said on live television that the scenes were the worst he had seen in more than 30 years.

Activities

In small groups, discuss the following questions.

1. Look at the picture of the children on their way to school. How do you feel about this picture?

2. Why might the Protestant residents have been so angry that Catholic parents were taking their children down that road?

3. What information would you like to have from both sides so you can get a better idea of why there was so much anger? Make a list of the questions you would like to ask.

4. Do you agree that children of different religions should go to different schools? Copy and complete a large table like the one below to show the advantages and the disadvantages of teaching children in separate schools.

Advantages	Disadvantages

5. There have been many events in Northern Ireland which have involved conflict between Catholics and Protestants. The trouble in Ardoyne is just one example. Some other examples are listed on this page.

   See if you can find out more about what happened in as many of these events as you can. Find out who was involved and the reasons for the conflict. Use the Internet (go to www.heinemann.co.uk/hotlinks) and your school or local library for your research.

   a Bloody Sunday.
   b Bloody Friday.
   c La Mon.
   d Enniskillen.
   e Teebane.
   f The Ormeau Betting Shop.
   g Omagh.

6. As a class, collect the questions which each group drew up for question 3. Try to contact a secondary school in Northern Ireland that may be able to answer your questions. Their school council would be a good starting point.

7. In the light of what you have found out, have you changed your original views about the battle of Holy Cross Infants School?

Extension activity

8. Use the Internet (go to www.heinemann.co.uk/hotlinks) to see if you can find out why the Ardoyne residents were so angry.

Getting technical

Conflict a fight or struggle.
Peace freedom from or the end of conflict or war.
Media this includes TV, radio, newspapers, magazines and the Internet.
War using weapons in a conflict.

● Save the Children

● Amnesty International

How does the media affect conflict?

Think about how we know what is happening around the world. How do we know about conflicts and the events caused by them? How do we know how these conflicts affect people? Most of us hear about these conflicts on television or on the radio. We read about them in newspapers and magazines. We can also use the Internet to find news and information. These are all different types of media.

But who controls the media, and who decides which stories to tell and which pictures to show? So many people rely on the media to let them know what is happening in the world that it can be a very powerful tool. It can change the way we feel about events simply by telling a story in a certain way.

The Vietnam War

The USA invaded Vietnam in March 1965 because it wanted to stop communist leaders from taking over Vietnam. The USA did not like communism – a form of government – and it wanted to stop it spreading around the world. The war went on until January 1973 and over two million people were killed. Many more were very badly injured.

Even though the USA had far better weapons and technology, it lost the war because the Vietnamese soldiers were better trained in fighting in the jungle. The war became very unpopular in the USA because so many people were being killed and injured, and because many people, even soldiers, were not really sure why they were fighting. The picture below, which was published in the USA soon after it happened, had a huge impact on the American public. It shows Vietnamese children who were burned by chemicals after an attack by US soldiers. It helped to turn public opinion against the war.

● How did the world media use this picture?

Public opinion when many people share the same views.

The Arab–Israeli conflict

Israel was a country set up for Jewish people in the Middle East in 1948. However, the land included areas that Palestinian Arab people claim is theirs. The two groups, Israelis and Palestinians, have been in conflict with each other ever since. In recent years, some Palestinian groups have used suicide bombers to kill Israeli civilians. Israel has attacked Palestinian areas, often leading to many people being killed.

The photograph of Muhammad-al-Durrah has been shown throughout the world. It made many people more aware of the trouble in Israel. It shows a 12-year-old Palestinian boy, (Muhammad al-Durrah), and his father. They were caught in the cross-fire between Israelis and Palestinians in the Gaza Strip in Israel. Even though the boy was being shielded by his father, he was killed. A French television crew caught the terrible incident on camera.

● Muhammad al-Durrah

Israel launches fresh Gaza attack

MAN DIES IN ISRAELI CAR BLAST

Children march for Palestine

Activities

1. What is meant by the term 'the media'?

2. Why is the media so powerful?

3. What does the term 'public opinion' mean?

4. Why is public opinion important?

5. Why do you think pictures of children in war situations can affect public opinion?

6. We have all experienced conflict with other people at some time in our lives. What advice would you give to anyone trying to resolve conflict peacefully?

Extension activities

7. Try to find out some opinions from sides of the Arab–Israeli conflict. Go to www.heinemann.co.uk/hotlinks and search the Internet to see how the views of some Jewish and Palestinian people differ. Are there any views that surprise you?

8. a Find another example of a conflict involving children. Try to find pictures of this conflict in the media. How might these pictures have affected public opinion?

   b Use the pictures you have found to carry out a survey. Ask a few people to describe how the pictures make them feel.

Reporting conflicts

We have seen how the media can affect the way we feel about conflict in the world. Now think about the people actually involved in the conflict. How can they tell their story?

Many people use art or writing to express the way they feel about conflict. They write poems, music or stories. They draw pictures and paint scenes. By doing this they can tell the story from their point of view. We can look at their work and get a sense of what it might have been like to be there too.

Most people would agree that conflict is good for nothing. However, because of the strong feelings caused by conflict, a number of people have produced some great works of art which show human suffering in the face of war.

Everywhere

Dig in boys for an extended stay
Those were the final words to come down that day
Waiting to be saved were the Philippines
You'll wait forever for the young Marines
Now I believe to be here is right
But I have to say I'm scared tonight
Crouching in this hole with a mouth full of sand
What comes first, the country or the man
Look at those slanted eyes coming up over the hill
Catching us by surprise, it's time to kill or be killed
Over here, over there, it's the same everywhere
A boy cries out for his mama before he dies for his home
All my life I wanted to be
As clever and strong as my best friend Lee
We grew up together along Half Moon Bay
Lee was Japanese, born in the USA
When Tommy was fighting Jerry along the River Seine
Me and Lee wanted to do the same
Then they bombed Pearl Harbor at the break of day
I was headed for these islands while Lee was hauled away
They said look at his slanted eyes, he's guilty as guilty can be
Sent here as enemy spies to sabotage the Land of the Free
I never got home, my platoon was never saved
That little fox hole became my island grave
Lee got out of jail but a prisoner he remained
Till he ended his own life to lose that ball and chain
And they said, Oh Little Slanted Eyes can't you forgive and forget
And he said, Oh Mr Friendly Ghost
Can you catch water in a net?

Words and music by Greg Trooper and Sid Griffin

Activities

Read the words to the song, *Everywhere*. In small groups, discuss the following questions.

1. Write down any lines in the song that you do not understand. Try to work out between you what these lines might mean.

2. Why would the marine be in a 'fox hole'?

3. What do you think the marine might have been feeling as he waited for the attack of the Japanese soldiers?

4. Why was Lee not allowed to join the marines like his friend?

5. Where do you think Lee and other Japanese Americans were 'hauled away' to?

6. What happened to the marine in the song?

7. What happened to Lee?

8. a. Why do you think Lee took his own life?
   b. What could have been done to stop him doing this?

Conflict – the past, present and future

September 11

On 11 September 2001, a group of terrorists hijacked four passenger planes in the USA. Two of the planes were deliberately flown into the Twin Towers of the World Trade Center in New York City. Both towers collapsed shortly afterwards, killing over 3,000 people including hundreds of emergency service workers who had gone inside to help.

The third hijacked plane crashed into the US military headquarters at the Pentagon in Washington. The fourth plane crashed in a field in the countryside.

The USA's FBI suspect a man called Osama bin Laden as being responsible for these attacks. He is head of a terrorist organization called Al-Qaeda, which is based in Afghanistan. This is an Islamic group, which means its members are Muslims. Islam is a popular religion in many Middle Eastern and Asian countries.

Since 11 September the USA and many other countries have been trying to find the leaders of Al-Qaeda to break up the organization.

In 2002 the USA announced that anybody visiting the country from countries such as Pakistan would have to be fingerprinted and investigated. People who do not have an Arabic appearance would just have to show their passports.

Activities

In small groups, discuss these questions.

1. How did you feel when you saw the 11 September attacks on television?

2. Which images of 11 September do you remember the most?

3. Did you take part in any type of fund-raising for the victims' families or send any condolences (cards, letters or e-mails)? If so, what did you do and how did you hope it might help the families?

4. Do you believe that it is right to treat all Arabic people differently because of these attacks? Explain your answer.

5. A stereotype is a simple description of a person which assumes that all people in a group will think and act in the same way. Why is it wrong to stereotype people?

Getting technical

Stereotype an unjustified and fixed standard image of a person.

How has 11 September affected some Muslim people?

There are many millions of Muslims in the world. The vast majority of Muslims were totally appalled by the attacks. But because of the actions of a small minority, a lot of Muslims are suffering. For example, the USA has changed the rules about some Muslims entering the country. Muslims in the UK and elsewhere have been attacked and discriminated against. This shows us that events taking place in one place can have an effect on people over the whole world. This is part of what is called 'globalisation'.

Case study 2

Under seige

Britain has a poor record for its treatment of Muslims. Since 11 September, for example, women wearing veils have been the target of violence and abuse.

On 11 September, a few hours after two hijacked planes crashed into the World Trade Center, a Muslim woman went to the doctor in Harrow, north London. 'You Muslims have done this!' the receptionist said in front of a packed waiting room. No one protested. The next day, a Muslim student in Glasgow got on a crowded bus. A white man moved to the seat behind her. 'You murderous Muslim,' he said, cracking a glass bottle over her head. Nobody helped her. The 20-year-old sat slumped and dazed until her next stop.
'The driver didn't do anything, even though he saw what had happened,' the victim said. 'It's a sad thing that, because of anti-Muslim feeling, no one came to my rescue.'

In the two months after 11 September, there were around 300 assaults on Muslims in Britain, and most of the victims were women.

Even before 11 September, many people in Britain behaved badly towards Muslims. The Runnymede Trust, a race relations group, produced a report on Islamophobia in the late 1990s, which, it claims, is still relevant today. The report found that Muslim communities suffered more from racist violence than any other minority communities in Britain.

Adapted from the *Guardian*, 8 December 2001

Getting technical

Islamophobia an unfounded fear of Muslims and anything Islamic.

Activities

1 Before US troops were sent to Afghanistan, President Bush called for a 'crusade'. Why might this word have upset Muslims around the world?

2 Read Case study 2.

   a According to the article, there has been an increase in attacks on Muslims since 11 September. Why do you think this is?

   b Some of the people in the article are stereotyping Muslims. How are they doing this?

   c What, in your opinion, can be done to help relations between Muslims and non-Muslims?

Extension activities

3 Find answers to the following questions about the Crusades to the Holy Land in the twelfth and thirteenth centuries.

Go to www.heinemann.co.uk/hotlinks and search the Internet and your school or local library for your research.

   a When did the Crusades happen?

   b Who was involved?

   c What were the motives of the Crusaders?

   d What did each the Crusaders and the Muslims do to each other?

4 Think of three ideas that could be used in your community to encourage better relations between Muslims and non-Muslims.

5 Contact a local mosque. Arrange to meet someone in charge to ask them about Islam and what their views are to establishing a peaceful world.

Some facts about Islam

The Qur'an, the holy book of Islam, contains these words about killing and suicide:

'Killing one innocent human being is like killing the entire human race'.

'Killing yourself [suicide] is forbidden in Islam and is an abuse of the divine gift of life'.

According to Islamic law, people who commit suicide are committing a major sin. Even the dying who may be in terrible pain are not allowed to wish death. The Prophet Muhammad said: 'Do not harm yourself or injure others.'

In the entire history of Islam – about 1,300 years – there are no examples of any mass murder or massacre.

When the Romans conquered a country, the first thing they did was to kill the people they defeated. When Muslims entered any country, they would give guarantees of life, property and honour to the defeated. Even in times of war, the Qur'an forbids Muslims to kill old people, women, children and those who are crippled or disabled.

Pakistani doubles star defiant

Pakistan's Aisam-Ul-Haq Qureshi insists he is not about to end his doubles partnership with Israeli Amir Hadad despite pressure from his country's sports officials.

Pakistan Sports Board condemned Qureshi for playing with an Israeli. Qureshi has been threatened with a ban if he continues to play with Hadad, but the Pakistani number one is not about to bow to the pressure.

'If I believe that I can win at the Grand Slams and the big events with Amir then I'll stay and play with him,' said Qureshi.

And he revealed that most of the press he was receiving in Pakistan was positive, although he will return home this week to face the music.

The Israeli makes no apologies for choosing to play with a Pakistani.

'I chose to play with him because of his talent, his skills as a tennis player, and I also like him as a person,' said Hadad.

Qureshi repeated the point that neither player talked about religion and both are happy to concentrate on tennis.

'I don't like religion or politics to interfere with sport,' he said. 'We're not here to change anything – politics and governments do that. We're just here to play the game and enjoy it.'

Activities

Read Case study 3.

1 Does the view of the Pakistani Sports Board surprise you?

2 Do you think it is possible for the two players to always avoid the subject of religion and to concentrate on tennis?

3 What are your thoughts on people from different religions working and playing together?

4 Newspapers and television help to form people's opinions. What have you read or seen which has helped to form your views about Islam?

What is peace?

The Nobel Prize for Peace

Every year in Norway a famous prize is given to people who are striving for peace. Here are some extracts from the speeches of people who have accepted the award.

A

I want to see Ireland as an example to men and women everywhere of what can be achieved by living for ideals, rather than fighting for them, and by viewing each and every person as worthy of respect and honour.

John Hume, the former leader of the Catholic Social Democratic Labour Party who has fought for peace and tolerance all his life

B

There are two traditions in Northern Ireland. There are two main religions. But there is only one future - and that is peace.

David Trimble, leader of the Ulster Unionist Party and First Minister of Northern Ireland who has condemned all terrorists in Northern Ireland

C

It is necessary to love peace and sacrifice for it. We must try not just to end war, but to make peace. We must see that peace represents a sweeter music.

Martin Luther King, an American civil rights leader who helped to give all black people the vote in the USA

D

This must be a world of democracy and respect for human rights. It must be a world freed from the horrors of poverty, hunger, deprivation and ignorance.

Nelson Mandela, former leader of the African National Congress who was imprisoned for over 27 years for being against the system of apartheid in South Africa

E

To live a full life, people must have the courage to bear the responsibility of the needs of others.

Aung San Suu Kyi, leader of Burma's opposition to the dictatorship in that country. She has been imprisoned and placed under house arrest to stop her expressing her views. Her speech was read by her son.

Activities

1 Think of a good definition for 'peace'.

2 Which of these extracts backs up your view about what peace is?

3 Which of these Nobel Prize winners for Peace have you heard of? What do you know about them?

4 Write a paragraph describing why peace is important and what peace means to you.

Extension activities

5 Find out about another Nobel Prize winner for Peace. Go to www.heinemann.co.uk/hotlinks and use the Internet and your school or local library for your research.
   a Why were they given the award?
   b What are their views about peace?
   c What are (or were) the circumstances of war or conflict in their countries?

6 Make a timeline or wall display about past winners of the Nobel Prize for Peace.

Review and reflect

In this chapter you have thought about and discussed these things:

- different views about peace
- why peace is so important
- how intolerance can lead to conflict
- things to help combat racial and religious intolerance
- how peace can be established.

Getting technical

Intolerance being unwilling or unable to put aside the beliefs of other people.

● Potential for Peace on Earth

● Burmese peace campaigners

Activities

1 Read the words to the song, *Peace on Earth*. In small groups, discuss the following questions.

   a What types of people are mentioned in the song?

   b Why might these people want peace?

2 **a** What other songs do you know about peace or war?

   b What do the words of these songs say about peace or war?

3 In about 100 words describe what an ideal country would be like. Explain how people would live together and treat each other.

4 What things could you do to help bring about peace in each of these situations?

   a The playground.

   b Your home.

   c The street where you live.

   d Your classes at school.

   e Helping people in another country.

Peace on Earth – U2

Heaven on Earth, we need it now
I'm sick of all this hanging around
Sick of sorrow, sick of pain
Sick of hearing again and again
That there's gonna be peace on Earth

Where I grew up there weren't many trees
Where there was we'd tear them down
And use them on our enemies
They say that what you mock
Will surely overtake you
And you became a monster
So the monster will not break you

It's already gone too far
Who said that if you go in hard
You won't get hurt?

Jesus can you take the time
To throw a drowning man a line
Peace on Earth
Tell the ones who hear no sound
Whose sons are living in the ground
Peace on Earth
No whos or whys
No one cries like a mother cries
For peace on Earth
She never got to say goodbye
To see the colour in his eyes
Now he's in the dirt
Peace on Earth

They're reading names out over the radio
All the folks the rest of us won't get to know
Sean and Julia, Gareth, Ann and Breda
Their lives are bigger than any big idea

Jesus can you take the time
To throw a drowning man a line
Peace on Earth
To tell the ones who hear no sound
Whose sons are living in the ground
Peace on Earth

Jesus sing a song you wrote
The words are sticking in my throat
Peace on Earth
Hear it every Christmas time
But hope and history won't rhyme
So what's it worth?
This peace on Earth

Peace on Earth
Peace on Earth
Peace on Earth

Index